Praise for *Taming Your Alpha Bitch*

"Self-acceptance is necessary before anyone can be happy. How wonderful that this book helps women stop torturing themselves emotionally, mentally, and physically, so that they can live in the bliss of love and prosperity."

—Terry Cole-Whittaker, #1 *New York Times* bestselling author of *What You Think of Me Is None of My Business*

"If you, like myself, desire a deeper and truer life, and a better understanding of yourself, this book will provide you with answers. I recommend this book for every woman who wants to step into her feminine power and create a life that truly works for her on EVERY level."

—Christine Kloser, author of *The Freedom Formula*

"A must-read for every woman who is tired of feeling frustrated, lonely, jealous, or emotionally tense. Rebecca and Christy show you how to achieve what you want while feeling more peaceful and connected. Highly recommended."

—Peggy McColl, *New York Times* bestselling author of *Your Destiny Switch*

"As a businesswoman, I have endured more than a few alpha bitches. This is a much-needed, overdue book I wish had been available to send to them. A must-read for both those who ARE alpha bitches and those who must work with them."

—Arielle Ford, *New York Times* bestselling author of *The Soulmate Secret*

"A great book for women interested in success, who are ready to take control of their financial futures and create lasting and sustainable wealth and power. Whitman and Grado illuminate the behaviors that women use to sabotage their financial health, while providing solid strategies for positive change."

—Loral Langemeier, CEO/founder of Live Out Loud, international speaker, money expert, and bestselling author of the Millionaire Maker three-book series and *Put More Cash in Your Pocket*

"A must-read for all over-controlling and over-doing achievement junkies who are tired of chasing balance and working so damn hard. *Taming Your Alpha Bitch* is a witty and wise guide that tells the truth about where our real power as women lies… and surprise, it's not where you think!"

—Christine Arylo, cofounder of Inner Mean Girl Reform School and author of *Choosing ME before WE*

"I applaud Christy Whitman and Rebecca Grado's new book on the divine feminine energy and the Law of Allowing. It comes in the right moment in time. Women will be back in power after thousands of years, to change life on Earth. This book is powerful because it teaches you how to unleash the power you are meant to have and be who you are meant to be."

—Dr. Carmen Harra, bestselling author of *The Trinity of Health*

"Expressing the masculine was something women needed to understand the feminine and sense, at a deeper level, how powerful and fulfilling living in the feminine is. This book shows you how to BE that fully embodied woman that you are. It is a primer for those of us turning more and more to embrace this wonderful and deep aspect of our being."

—Jennifer McLean, healer, speaker, author, and host of "Healing with the Masters"

"*Taming Your Alpha Bitch* is so important. So many women, myself included, know the stress that comes from the forceful, competitive, masculine inner-drive, but true feminine strength is not that at all—it's wise, collaborative, receptive, creative, and intuitive. This is the true power of women. Bravo for bringing us such a book!"

—Colette Baron-Reid, internationally renowned intuitive counselor, educator, and bestselling author of *The Map: Finding the Magic and Meaning in the Story of Your Life*

"When you read this book, you will see that there really are only two choices in any situation—the hard way or the easy way. *Taming Your Alpha Bitch* will help you discover what's lurking underneath your Alpha female so you can manifest your desires from your peaceful and pure feminine power—bringing more joy, fulfilling relationships, and effortless success. In essence, you'll learn how to make things easy. And who doesn't want that?"

—Beth A. Grant, marketing strategist and award-winning writer and editor

"An informative, fantastic book! I give a standing ovation to the authors. Bravo!"

—Lisa Whatley, self-help empowerment specialist, published writer, life coach, and energy medicine healer

Taming Your

ALPHA
BITCH

Taming Your
ALPHA
BITCH

How to be Fierce AND Feminine (and Get Everything You Want)

REBECCA GRADO, M.S., MFT
& CHRISTY WHITMAN

BenBella Books, Inc.
Dallas, Texas

BenBella

BenBella Books, Inc.
10300 N. Central Expressway, Suite 400
Dallas, TX 75231
www.benbellabooks.com • Send feedback to feedback@benbellabooks.com

Printed in the United States of America
10 9 8 7 6 5 4 3 2 1

Library of Congress Cataloging-in-Publication Data
Grado, Rebecca.
Taming your alpha bitch : how to be fierce and feminine (and get everything you want) / Rebecca Grado and Christy Whitman. p. cm.
Includes bibliographical references and index. ISBN 978-1-936661-15-2 (alk. paper)
1. Assertiveness in women. 2. Women--Psychology. I. Whitman, Christy. II. Title.
HQ1206.G737 2011
155.3'3336--dc23
2011034827

Editing by Sara Cassidy
Copyediting by Lisa Miller
Proofreading by Michael Fedison
Cover design by Kit Sweeney
Text design and composition by Silver Feather Design
Printed by Berryville Graphics

Distributed by Perseus Distribution • www.perseusdistribution.com
To place orders through Perseus Distribution:
Tel: 800-343-4499
Fax: 800-351-5073
E-mail: orderentry@perseusbooks.com

Significant discounts for bulk sales are available. Please contact Glenn Yeffeth at glenn@benbellabooks.com or (214) 750-3628.

Table of Contents

Introduction 1

chapter one
The Forceful Alpha 21

chapter two
The Controlling Alpha 53

chapter three
The Competitive Alpha 97

chapter four
The Disruptive Alpha 133

chapter five
The Driving Force behind
All Alpha Behaviors 165

conclusion
From Alpha Bitch to Femininely
Empowered Woman 195

Acknowledgments 205

About the Authors 209

Introduction

Now more than any other moment in history, we as women are discovering and expressing the full magnitude of our authentic, unabashed power. After hundreds of years of biting our tongues, biding our time, and batting our eyelashes, we've finally hung up our aprons and bid farewell to the submissive "damsel in distress" role that has served as both an archetype and a stereotype of what it means to be feminine.

Take a look at the shifting global landscape and you'll see that women are advancing to the forefront of almost every industry. We are successful entrepreneurs, CEOs of Fortune 500 companies, influential leaders, and respected, contributing members of our communities. We have broken through glass ceilings, leveled career and educational playing fields, and proven beyond a shadow of a doubt that we can generate our own prosperity. We're even taking our rightful place in politics, not only as first ladies but also as vice presidential candidates and prospective commanders in chief.

This newfound surge of power isn't confined solely to the workplace, either. We're also taking a more assertive role in our personal relationships, successfully (and often single-

handedly) running our households and making key decisions on everything from child care to financial investments.
We are now firmly established in territory that was strictly
off-limits to us just a few decades ago; as a result, more choices and opportunities are open to us than ever before.

Yes, ladies, we have rightfully earned the social, eco-
nomic, and political equality that we've been fighting for
more than 100 years to achieve. And we have definitely
seized every opportunity to prove that we have what it takes
to succeed in a "man's" world (and oh, have we proved it).

In the span of just two generations, our accomplishments as women have led to some pretty impressive break-
throughs...and some unprecedented break*downs*. Along
with our expanded options, many of us are feeling more
anxious, exhausted, overwhelmed, and out of balance—
both within ourselves and in our relationships with others.

As female empowerment experts, we meet thousands
of women each year—in our counseling and coaching practices, at conferences, and during our Goddess Retreats (a
transformational weekend that awakens the radiance, mystery, and power within each
woman)—and an alarming
number of them report feeling more stress than ease,
and having more moments
of frustration than delight.
Despite the wealth of opportunities at their fingertips,
many women are experienc-
ing the "glass half empty"

*Despite the wealth of
opportunities at their
fingertips, many women are
experiencing the "glass half
empty" feeling in areas of
their lives where they yearn
for abundance.*

feeling in areas of their lives where they yearn for abundance. It's certainly not a lack of intelligence, strength, or determination that's preventing these amazing women— and perhaps you as well—from creating the fulfillment they seek. In fact, many of those we've coached and counseled over the years are strong, competent women who have attained a high degree of success in their lives. And, like them, you may be wondering why, given this success, you're feeling unfulfilled, dissatisfied, or downright depleted.

At times, managing all the different roles we play can feel a bit like performing a complicated circus act; eventually one of the plates we've been working so hard to keep spinning will come crashing to the ground. It seems that the moment we achieve mastery in one area of our lives, things fall apart in another. Just when our careers are cruising along at full speed, we realize that our sex lives have broken down by the side of the road. Or perhaps we've finally managed to create a sense of balance at home and a strong connection with our families, but wake up one morning to discover that we can't button our slacks. This imbalance leaves us lost between feelings of complete exhilaration and utter powerlessness. Common scenarios like these suggest that while we most certainly have "come a long way, baby," we still have a ways to go to create the 100 percent fulfillment and core-deep empowerment we seek.

Since most of us were raised in a largely male-dominated culture, where examples of powerful and successful men far outnumbered those of powerful, successful women, we naturally adopted a masculine approach to fulfilling our life goals. It just made sense, right? If we wanted to enjoy the same degree of empowerment that most men did, we had to seize that power, just like a man. As a result, many of us said "so long" to the familiar role of "helpless fairy-tale heroine" and donned a cutthroat, ambitious, and competitive stance. Summoning all the machisma we could muster, we forged ahead, determined to take by force everything we longed to achieve.

Time for a New Method

The masculine approach to success has served us well and was a necessary step in our evolution, but thanks to the generations of women who came before us, we are now poised to take the next step toward the realization of our full *feminine* power. Like the women who struggled to find their voices before us, we are now feeling a growing urgency to awaken all of our latent potential and experience a deeper connection to ourselves, to others, and to life itself.

The masculine approach to success has served us well and was a necessary step in our evolution, but . . . we are now poised to take the next step toward the realization of our full feminine power.

We sense there is something more within us that is yearning to be expressed and want more than anything to make the leap from mediocrity to excellence. At some level, we know that we have the potential to be wildly successful—not just in one area of life but in all of them. We deserve to have a thriving career, financial abundance, physical vitality, emotional fulfillment, adventure, romance, and anything else our hearts desire. So when we find ourselves coming up short of our full potential in any area, it's only natural for us to feel discontent that ranges from mild apathy to intense frustration.

And what do most of us strong, determined women do to alleviate this discontent? We work harder, of course! We roll up our sleeves, strengthen our resolve, and pursue our goals more aggressively. In other words, we adopt the mindset, the attitude, and the tactics of a dominant, pushy woman (one who some call an Alpha Bitch).

Barking up the Wrong Tree: The Alpha Bitch Approach to Life and Love

What exactly is an Alpha Bitch? In the animal kingdom, the "alpha" is the most dominant member of the pack, the one that outranks all the rest and will literally fight to the death for the right to retain her top spot. And, of course, we're all familiar with the derogatory implications of a woman who is called a "bitch"—her behavior is characterized as aggressive, spiteful, disruptive, or malicious. The Alpha Bitch, like her canine counterpart, is power driven and struggles for dominance. She pursues her goals with a forceful, aggressive, "take no prisoners" approach. And she will use whatever it takes—including overbearing, controlling, competitive, and disruptive behaviors—to prove her importance and protect her hard-earned status. No doubt you've crossed paths with an Alpha Bitch or found yourself a bit "Alpha Bitch" inclined from time to time?

When we're operating in Alpha Bitch mode, we actually believe the only way we can get our needs met is by dominating and controlling the people and circumstances in our lives. Instead of basking in and benefiting from the resources that are all around us, our inner Alpha Bitch generates an almost perpetual feeling of isolation and disconnection—a "me against the world" mentality. If we want anything done right we'll have to do it ourselves, and if we don't hold everything together it will surely fall apart. We're convinced that the kids won't eat, the bills won't get paid, and the earth just won't rotate properly on its axis unless we are the ones directing it. Of course, this perception weighs heavily on our shoulders, sending us spiraling into overwhelm, furrowing our brows, closing down our hearts, and literally draining the joy out of our lives. Trying to claim our personal power by assuming an Alpha Bitch mindset is, ironically, disempowering. The more forcefully we push to achieve our desires, the more distance we end up creating between ourselves and the extraordinary lives we envision.

Trying to claim our personal power by assuming an Alpha Bitch mindset is, ironically, disempowering. The more forcefully we push to achieve our desires, the more distance we end up creating between ourselves and the extraordinary lives we envision.

Now, you might be wondering why the masculine approach gets a man what he wants but ultimately works against a woman. The simple answer is that men and women are wired differently. Men work best by exerting bursts of full-out energy, while women are designed to evenly distribute their energy at a steady pace for longer periods of time. Men are built for sprinting; women for marathons. Biologically, this makes perfect sense. In more primitive times, men needed huge bursts of energy to take down their prey; and once they bagged their kill, their work was done and they could rest. (And, ladies, we're all familiar with the resting habits of men, right?) Women, on the other hand, needed endurance to keep the home fires burning, to prepare the food, and to care for their young.

Today, most of us find ourselves managing responsibilities at home and in our communities, and working more than just the typical eight-hour day. If we take a masculine, forceful, "get-it-done" approach to these tasks it's only a matter of time before we'll burn out. We may get the results we want in the short term but at a great cost to our physical and emotional well-being. When our efforts to succeed are out of alignment with our true nature, our emotions become unsettled and our end results less accomplished. In other words, the way men go about attaining their goals is not necessarily the one we should emulate when seeking to attain ours. What you'll learn in our book are methods that will serve you much more effectively to bring you the success you desire, while honoring your natural feminine rhythm.

Now just to be clear, we are not denying the fact that playing the role of the Alpha Bitch commands attention and makes things happen. There are definitely situations

Although it's nice to know that we can summon our inner warrior when needed, it's counterproductive to charge through life with weapons perpetually drawn.

where channeling our inner she-wolf is absolutely necessary—defending ourselves against harm and protecting the well-being of our children are two that immediately come to mind. But it is important to recognize those moments when we need to be fight-ready are usually few and far between. Although it's nice to know that we can summon our inner warrior when needed, it's counterproductive to charge through life with weapons perpetually drawn.

The Stressful Life of the Alpha

On the whole, American society subscribes to the belief that to realize our full potential we need intense ambition, hard work, a fierce attitude, and a forceful will. If this value system were written as an equation, it would go something like this: *the greater the effort, the better the outcome.* And while this may work in some specific instances and for males, it turns out that the whole nose-to-the-grindstone approach has brought women more than just accomplishments and recognition— our noses have gotten a bit bloody in the process.

The Alpha Bitch mentality is harsh and demanding, and sometimes we are hardest on ourselves. This critical attitude creates resistance in our bodies, and a body in resistance is a body in pain. When we are being forceful and demeaning with ourselves (instead of loving and accepting) we may find our health deteriorating, as well as our relationships with others.

Studies in animal behavior have shown that a dog, wolf, or primate who establishes him or herself as the "alpha" of the pack has a significantly shorter life span than those who rank lower on the social hierarchy. There may be a variety of reasons for this, but one compelling theory is that because the alpha animal is always "on," the stress that accumulates over time eventually causes his or her body to break down. By constantly forcing and controlling, we alpha humans place our bodies and minds under undue stress, making us susceptible to illness and disease. Long-term exposure to stress disrupts every system in our bodies and can lead to serious health problems. It can raise blood pressure, suppress the immune system, increase the risk of heart attack and stroke, contribute to infertility, and accelerate the aging process. Chronic stress can even rewire the brain, leaving us more vulnerable to anxiety and depression.

With this intensely stressful lifestyle comes every woman's least-favorite side effect—weight gain! When the constant, crazy demands we put on ourselves stress us out, our cortisol levels rise, slowing our metabolisms. As if a slow metabolism isn't bad enough, when we feel depleted many of us reach for fatty, sugary foods that are high in calories. Late-night freezer raids to get Ben & Jerry's ice cream may feel good now, but we are really just masking (with tasty treats) the bigger problems—we are out of our true feminine alignment and feeling undernourished. Wielding Alpha Bitch force creates undue stress on a female body, wastes a lot of energy, and negatively affects us in so many ways. In fact, when it becomes our *habitual* way of relating to the world, the results we reap are ultimately unfulfilling because we sacrifice intimacy, synergy, and our connection to others (and ourselves) in the process of aggressively going after what we want.

For example, our more cutthroat tactics may have won us promotions at work, but do our office mates respect us or invite us to join them for an after-work martini? Also, our ultimatums and bossiness may check items off our "honey do" list, but do our husbands still look at us with adoring eyes? The "drill sergeant" routine we use to keep our households running shipshape might get things done, but are our children eager to hang out with us? Our friends may include us for "girls' night out," but do they trust us enough to share their true feelings?

Employees and colleagues may appear supportive when under our watchful eyes, but they are quick to undermine or even sabotage us when we're not around to police them. Family members and friends may smile politely when in our presence, but do their best to avoid us altogether, scattering like mice in order to steer clear of our scrutiny or criticism.

Approaching life in an Alpha Bitch manner ultimately works *against* us because it introduces conflict, struggle, and competition to our personal and professional relationships—leaving us feeling even more isolated and overwhelmed. And here's the biggest downfall: operating from this mindset does more than raise our blood pressure and make us appear tense or on edge; it directly affects our ability to create the life we desire by *energetically* blocking us from receiving the abundance we deserve. How? Well, it turns out that the aggressive, masculine demeanor that we thought would place us on the fast track to success is actually driven by the underlying beliefs of fear and lack—and these beliefs have a lot to do with the results we ultimately create. Let's break this down.

The Law of Attraction

Everything we attract into our lives—whether we're experiencing struggle or ease, scarcity or abundance, frustration or fulfillment—is the direct result of what we believe to be true about ourselves, others, and the world. Our core beliefs direct our thoughts, and our thoughts cause us to experience specific feelings. Our feelings, together with our thoughts, influence our energy ... and it's our energy that draws to us the outcomes we experience.

What do we mean by "energy"? We live in a vibrationally based universe. Everything, from this book you are reading to the thoughts you are thinking, carries a particular energy or vibrational frequency. Scientists call these vibrations "strings" of energy. According to quantum physics, we are constantly projecting these measurable energetic frequencies or vibrations out into the universe and receiving *similar* energies in response. The frequency at which our energy resonates influences our life experiences.

Now if this scientific definition left your head spinning, don't worry. All you really need to understand is that *everything is energy* (including you), and your energetic "vibes" determine the results you create in life. The following Manifestation Formula illustrates exactly how this process works:

MANIFESTATION FORMULA

Beliefs → Thoughts → Feelings = Energy → Outcome

The thoughts, beliefs, and feelings we experience on a moment-to-moment basis have a powerful and immediate influence on our personal "frequency" or energy field. Like a radio signal, our vibration is transmitted to the far corners of the universe, and the universe responds by magnetizing to us other people, circumstances, and experiences that are consistent with that vibration. For example, if you have a core belief that you are inadequate, this belief will inform your thoughts, fueling an internal dialogue that might go something like this: *I'll never be as smart as my friends. Who would ever find me attractive? Nobody would want to hire me. Why am I always screwing up?* These thoughts then affect your feelings, most likely leaving you in a depressed, down-in-the-dumps kind of mood. As your energetic vibration plummets, this lower frequency is broadcast, invisibly but powerfully into the universe, attracting to you life experiences that mirror the same low energetic vibration. On the other hand, beliefs that are aligned with principles such as abundance, balance, collaboration, and self-acceptance generate a calm and harmonious frequency that enables us to create what we desire, with less struggle and greater joy.

The results we draw to ourselves—the quality of our relationships, our level of vitality, and the degree of abundance and satisfaction we experience in our careers—all provide feedback about the nature of the relationship we have with the universe. Whatever life experiences we receive are a direct reflection of the energy we send out. This is the essence of the Law of Attraction, and the secret behind all manifestation.

Whatever life experiences we receive are a direct reflection of the energy we send out. This is the essence of the Law of Attraction, and the secret behind all manifestation.

The powerful Law of Attraction is at the root of everything that you experience; and the stable, never-changing, always-accurate premise of this *Law* is: *that which is like unto itself, is drawn.**

—Abraham-Hicks

* Esther and Jerry Hicks, *The Vortex* (Carlsbad, CA: Hay House), 19.

Beliefs are like magnets; they draw to us everything we experience in our reality. And although it may try to camouflage itself as confidence and superiority, the Alpha

Bitch attitude is set into motion by core beliefs of fear and insufficiency. These beliefs change our vibration from calm and harmonious to chaotic and competitive, keeping our dreams perpetually out of reach.

The good news is that through awareness and subsequent action (which begins with a new attitude and approach), we can shift our energy and vibrate at a higher, brighter level that will draw more positive outcomes to us. So, how do we get from where we are to where we want to be?

From Alpha Bitch to Femininely Empowered Woman: Applying the Laws of the Universe to Bring About Change

Before we can effectively tame our Alpha Bitch tendencies, it's important to acknowledge that we started acting this way for a reason. Think of the modern Alpha Bitch as a sort of natural adaptation—a necessary step in our evolution as women. Trading in the helpless "damsel in distress" archetype for that of the Alpha Bitch was not a mistake or a setback but a vital and necessary step in our ongoing quest for empowerment. In the same way that learning to crawl is an essential step in learning how to walk, we had to realize that we *are* powerful before we could learn how to wield that power wisely. But just like the baby who one day discovers that toddling will take her farther than crawling, we have reached the outer limits of how far our heavy-handed tactics can advance us. The reign of the Alpha Bitch is rapidly coming to an end simply because we've already learned all the lessons she can teach.

We're all familiar with Charles Darwin's "Survival of the Fittest" theory, which asserts that in a world of limited resources, only those who prove themselves most capable of enduring the struggle for existence will ultimately survive. Less than a hundred years after Darwin published this famous theory, biologist Jonas Salk declared that it was already obsolete, arguing that it's not the "fittest" who survive, but the *wisest*. We no longer live in a "dog eat dog" world; the people who have it all—outer success and inner fulfillment—are not necessarily the biggest or the strongest (or the pushiest) but those who are wise enough to embrace universal principles.

Tapping into our inner Alpha Bitch caused us to realize that women are as equal, capable, and entitled to lead lives of influence and greatness as any man. It gave us permission to bare our teeth when necessary and the ambition to boldly go after our desires. We know how to fend for ourselves, how to fight for our rights, and how to claw our way to the top. Thanks to her, we know how to survive. Now it's time for us to learn how to *thrive*—to enjoy the success we've worked so hard to attain, while reaping maximum fulfillment in our lives.

> *We don't have to reject our femininity in order to succeed. We can call on our masculine strength when necessary, while remaining true to our feminine nature. In doing so, we integrate both energies and harness their collective creative power.*

Making the shift from Alpha Bitch to Femininely Empowered Woman begins with the realization that we don't have to reject our femininity in order to succeed. We can call on our masculine strength when necessary, while remaining true to our feminine nature. In doing so, we integrate both energies and harness their collective creative power.

As you begin to understand and apply the universal laws that we'll introduce you to throughout this book—the laws of Pure Potentiality, Allowing, Oneness, Balance and Harmony, and Sufficiency and Abundance—you'll naturally release the outworn Alpha Bitch mentality. You'll learn that the more forcefully you go after your desires, the more distance you'll create between yourself and that desire. And you will see how living in fear directly blocks you from creating the abundance you desire and deserve. Most importantly, you'll learn how it's your energy, not just your effort, that brings to you all that you experience in life.

In each chapter, we'll show you that your energy is affected by one of these four common Alpha Bitch behaviors: force, control, competition, and disruption, and how these behaviors arise from underlying beliefs of lack and fear. We'll also show you the five keys that place you in perfect alignment with your femininity, gracefully unlocking doors to abundance that are impossible to open by force.

You'll learn how cultivating qualities like inspiration, tranquility, trust, and fulfillment sets the universal laws into motion in your life, enabling you to more easily attract the things you desire—not through painstaking hard work or coercion, but through the sheer power of your magnetism. When you are in touch with the power that resides at your core, rather than seeking to dominate others by imposing your outward will, you radiate a kind of quiet elegance. You command attention, not through loud words or disruptive behaviors, but through graciousness and self-confidence. Because you treat others with respect and care, you draw people in, naturally eliciting their cooperation and support.

When you identify something you want, you will, of course, invest time and energy to bring it to fruition, but you'll remain mindful that your real power to manifest what you want must be activated from within. By radiating clarity and certainty—two very powerful determinants in attracting—you'll begin to *find yourself more and more at the right place at the right time* and *things coming to you with greater ease.*

As a Femininely Empowered Woman, you'll finally be able to relinquish the "lone wolf" mentality that makes you think that you need to do everything by yourself. Instead, you'll have the humility and the faith to turn to an extended tribe of people with whom you can collaborate and cocreate, trusting in a field of intelligence greater than yourself to guide and provide for you in every situation. As the sensations of overwhelm and struggle are replaced by feelings of awe and gratitude, life will be so much easier.

We have certainly worked hard for every bit of success we've earned. Now it's time we reap that success through an easier method, one that is less taxing, more fruitful, and a whole lot more fun!

Let Us Lead You There

As a licensed psychotherapist with more than twenty-five years of professional experience in guiding and empowering women (Rebecca), and a certified Law of Attraction coach who regularly addresses audiences nationwide on these topics (Christy), we'll guide you through hands-on, experiential exercises to activate your feminine power and generate immediate and tangible changes in your life. Be prepared to:

- experience a shift in consciousness that trickles all the way down to the thoughts, feelings, choices, and attitudes that permeate your day-to-day reality;
- attract the resources required to live an abundant and magical life;
- be more effective: get more done in less time with less stress;
- experience your true power at a core-deep level;
- approach life in a calm, balanced, and harmonious way;
- cultivate a deeper connection to your wise, all-knowing self;
- release all obstacles and limiting beliefs that stand in your way;
- experience more joy, enthusiasm, confidence, and freedom; and
- awaken your true feminine power so that your visions, ideas, and dreams effortlessly become your reality.

And you'll do it all with a sense of grace, without denying your inherent power or wielding it like a weapon.

Almost involuntarily you'll adopt a more evolved and integrated approach to life: from wielding force to embodying power; from controlling to allowing; from competing to collaborating; from being disruptive and dramatic to becoming balanced and harmonious; from a mindset of lack and limitation to one of sufficiency and abundance; and ultimately, from a life that is based in fear to one that is overflowing with love.

If you're ready to start putting these laws to work in your favor, then read on.

chapter one
The Forceful Alpha

"The details of your incompetence do not interest me," snarls Miranda Priestly in the 2006 film *The Devil Wears Prada*. Priestly (brilliantly played by Oscar-winning actress Meryl Streep) is the personification of a Forceful Alpha Bitch. *She is a berating, dismissive, hard-edged woman whose tongue cuts like a deadly weapon. She may be dressed to the nines, but she is a ruthless ballbuster who clawed her way to the top and stops at nothing to make sure she stays there.* In both her personal and professional lives, Priestly rules with the proverbial iron fist. And although she makes quite a name for herself in the industry, her caustic attitude breeds hatred and pushes others away, eventually even alienating her husband.

If only this variety of Alpha Bitch were merely a fictional character depicted on the big screen, but alas, that's just not the case. We've all had the, um, *pleasure* of standing behind a Forceful Alpha in the department store checkout line, cringing as she barks out demands and reduces sales clerks to tears with her condescending tone. We've dodged her grocery cart as she motors down the aisles, unconcerned that she's plowing over others' toes. We've been shoved aside in restaurants as she charges the hostess stand without a thought about the hungry families who've been patiently waiting for their tables. We've averted our eyes, kept our mouths shut, and deliberately avoided her whenever she's crossed our paths. This woman seems perpetually on edge and poised to unleash her fury at any moment, so it's best to just stay out of her way. That is, unless you have to work or live with her.

Her motto in the office is, "A good employee is a submissive employee." She is the boss from hell who steamrolls over her coworkers' ideas and opinions, not to mention their feelings, leaving a trail of flattened roadkill in her wake. Challenge her in any way and she'll target you relentlessly—humiliating you in meetings, rejecting your ideas, and squashing any hopes of advancing.

She is the stuff relationship nightmares are made of: punitive, punishing, and pejorative. Maybe it's her condescending tone or the intimidating glare she's perfected that reduces her partner to a driveling "yes man." In her presence, even successful, accomplished men may find themselves taking cues from the family dog, who beats a quick path to his kennel the minute he hears her walk through the front door.

As a mom she's overbearing and, at times, humiliating. She has no qualms telling her child's karate instructor—loudly and in the middle of class—how to do his job (never mind that *sensei* is a fourth-degree black belt). The Forceful Alpha mom will bully her children's nannies, teachers, Cub Scout masters, and playmates' parents if they challenge her in any way. She'll walk all over her kids, too. Disciplining and dominating are words that often get confused in her mind.

The Forceful Alpha is the friend who seems to think she's doing others a favor by allowing them to do things for her. Petrified of winding up on her bad side, the members of her unofficial entourage find themselves toting her kids around town, picking up her dry cleaning, and delivering her daily half-caf skinny latte with no foam and extra Splenda. She is the know-it-all sister, mother-in-law, and neighbor who insists on having everything her way. On a good day, she comes across as a powerful, assertive woman who knows what she wants and how to articulate it clearly. But when her take-charge attitude is fueled by force, rather than authentic power, she becomes domineering and aggressive to the point of infringing on the rights and freedoms of others.

> On a good day, she comes across as a powerful, assertive woman who knows what she wants and how to articulate it clearly. But when her take-charge attitude is fueled by force rather than authentic power, she becomes domineering and aggressive to the point of infringing on the rights and freedoms of others.

Convinced of her importance, she may unintentionally (or intentionally) dismiss or disregard others' opinions. Even the way this woman carries herself when she walks into a room seems to repel support and empathy while inciting conflict—especially from other women. Her preoccupation with her own agenda has stripped her of customary graciousness and everyday acts of kindness. In short, the Forceful Alpha has not yet learned how to play nice with others. For this woman, the ends justify almost any means and she's willing to throw others under the bus to get her way.

We've certainly run across women like this from time to time, and it's easy to dismiss this behavior as something that *other* gals do. Although it's probably safe to say that most of us stop short of these over-the-top antics, if we're being honest with ourselves, we'll admit that we've "gone there" a time or two. We've unleashed our inner Forceful Alpha on some unsuspecting person, perhaps not as aggressively as Miranda Priestly, but aggressively nonetheless.

Every now and then we've crossed the line from strong and assertive to dominant and aggressive. Maybe, after a stressful day at work, we've barked at the grocery store clerk who was moving too slowly. Or perhaps our husband was trying to be playful, but was really just distracting, so we snapped at him with a small offhanded comment. Or maybe a coworker wasn't "dialed in" during a meeting, so a little glare her way let her know we meant business.

Sometimes it's the edge in our voice or "the look" we give that warns others to back off or pull it together *fast!* Because our subtle ways of being pushy aren't blatantly offensive, they may not register on our radar as forceful. But don't be too quick to write off the Forceful Alpha as "so *not* me." You might be surprised to find that there are Forceful Alpha tendencies in many strong, successful women (yourself included).

If you are starting to question whether you might be a Forceful Alpha, take the following quiz and see where you rank:

THE FORCEFUL FEMME FATALE—ARE YOU THIS TYPE OF ALPHA BITCH?

1. *When your husband admits he's having a hard time completing a home improvement project that you've been looking forward to for weeks, you . . .*

    A   Try to understand the problem so you can brainstorm possible solutions.
    B   Unleash your pent-up fury on him at his inability to get things done!
    C   Listen to his concern and ask what, if anything, you can do to help.
    D   Shift it into high gear—you're going to have to take over this whole operation!

2. *At a staff meeting, an intern comes forward with what is clearly an ill-conceived idea. As her supervisor, you . . .*

    A   Acknowledge the effort while offering down-to-earth feedback.
    B   Steamroll right over it. This is not amateur hour!
    C   Politely thank her for sharing, but roll your eyes at your colleagues to signal your disapproval.
    D   Wait until the meeting concludes, then admonish her for not running her idea by you first.

3. *Realizing that you have an appointment on the day you're scheduled to drive your kids' carpool, you . . .*

    A   Call the other mom. Naturally, she'll cover your shift.

continued on next page . . .

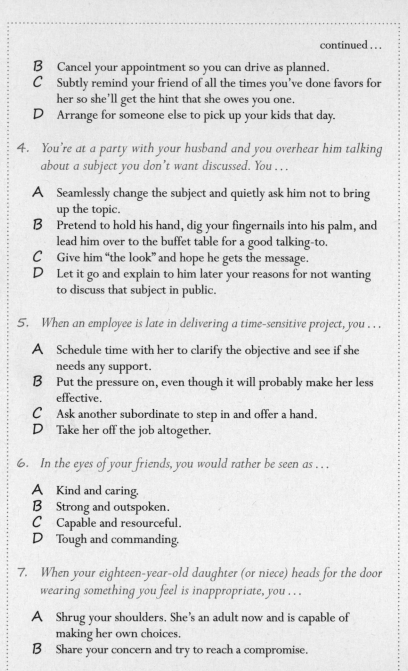

continued ...

B   Cancel your appointment so you can drive as planned.
C   Subtly remind your friend of all the times you've done favors for her so she'll get the hint that she owes you one.
D   Arrange for someone else to pick up your kids that day.

4. *You're at a party with your husband and you overhear him talking about a subject you don't want discussed. You ...*

A   Seamlessly change the subject and quietly ask him not to bring up the topic.
B   Pretend to hold his hand, dig your fingernails into his palm, and lead him over to the buffet table for a good talking-to.
C   Give him "the look" and hope he gets the message.
D   Let it go and explain to him later your reasons for not wanting to discuss that subject in public.

5. *When an employee is late in delivering a time-sensitive project, you ...*

A   Schedule time with her to clarify the objective and see if she needs any support.
B   Put the pressure on, even though it will probably make her less effective.
C   Ask another subordinate to step in and offer a hand.
D   Take her off the job altogether.

6. *In the eyes of your friends, you would rather be seen as ...*

A   Kind and caring.
B   Strong and outspoken.
C   Capable and resourceful.
D   Tough and commanding.

7. *When your eighteen-year-old daughter (or niece) heads for the door wearing something you feel is inappropriate, you ...*

A   Shrug your shoulders. She's an adult now and is capable of making her own choices.
B   Share your concern and try to reach a compromise.

C Show your disapproval by making an offhanded remark like, "Where do you think you're going dressed like that, young lady?"

D Put your foot down. She's changing her clothes or she's not going anywhere.

8. *While backing out of a parking lot, you tap fenders with someone who was backing out at the exact same moment. You get out to survey the damage, and . . .*

A Make sure no one was hurt.

B Demand the other driver's insurance information immediately; clearly it was her fault!

C Give her your insurance information, but let her know that you're now late to your next appointment because of her poor driving skills.

D Let it go because clearly you were both at fault.

9. *When one member of your team at work turns in an assignment that you feel is not up to par, you . . .*

A Send it back and tell her that it's unacceptable. You're on a deadline and don't have time to mince words!

B Put in the extra effort to improve it and let her know that you are disappointed in her effort.

C Acknowledge the things she did well and as clearly as possible articulate the things that need improvement.

D Complain to your superior and demand that she be pulled from the project.

10. *Your partner hasn't quite figured out what you like in bed. You decide to . . .*

A Patiently and playfully teach him.

B Leave a dog-eared, highlighted copy of *The Joy of Sex* lying around where he's sure to see it. Maybe he'll get the hint.

C Wait until the next time you make love and then give him step-by-step instructions, like a flight tower bringing a jet in for landing.

continued on next page . . .

continued...

D Talk about your likes and dislikes when you're not in the heat of passion so he'll be less defensive and more receptive.

SCORING KEY:

1. a-2, b-5, c-1 d-4 • 2. a-1, b-5, c-3, d-4 • 3. a-5, b-1, c-3, d-2 • 4. a-1, b-5, c-4, d-1 • 5. a-1, b-4, c-3, d-5 6. a-1, b-3, c-2, d-5 • 7. a-1, b-2, c-4, d-5 • 8. a-1, b-5, c-4, d-1 • 9. a-4, b-3, c-1, d-5 • 10. a-1, b-3, c-5, d-2

ASSESSMENT:

Using the number that corresponds to each answer you gave, add up the total number of points.

If you scored 20 or fewer points, you understand that honey catches more flies than vinegar and you use real power, rather than force, to make things happen.

If you scored between 21 and 35 points, you are a strong woman who can spur others to action; however, it's highly likely that you're stepping on a few toes in the process and that your accomplishments are at the expense of other people's feelings.

If you scored between 35 and 50 points, you've probably confused power with force. In the short term you may like the fact that people bend to your will but in the long run, the way you interact with them can create an atmosphere of fear, tension, or intimidation. Read on to discover how aligning with the Law of Pure Potentiality can bring about even better results by utilizing the fluid, magnetic, feminine qualities of ease and grace.

The Pit Bull or the Poodle—Is There a Third Option?

There must be something in the water, because more and more of us are approaching our education, our careers, and even our love lives with this harsh "pit bull" kind of attitude. In ways that are both blatant and subtle, we've gotten the message that only hard-hitting, tough gals get the success and respect they deserve. If we want love, we have to aggressively pursue promising options. If we want a thriving career, we have to bulldoze our way through the competition to create it. In essence, if we're going to get anywhere in this world, we had better learn how to throw our weight around like a man, because let's face it, soft and feminine might get us dates, but it won't get us the big office on the top floor, right? It seems that our only two choices are the pit bull that gets what she wants, or the poodle that's cute and cuddly but lacks the chops to be effective.

We've certainly seen our fair share of hyper-aggressive females who take what they want by force—just check out the reality television series *The Real Housewives* of Atlanta, New York, New Jersey, Orange County, Beverly Hills, and Miami. (In fact, Miranda Priestly is relatively tame compared to some of those table-flipping, hair-pulling, name-calling socialites!) Say what we will about them, but they certainly seem to have prestige and power. And we also know plenty of "feminine" women as well, like our sweet Aunt Patsy, and maybe the lovely elementary school librarian. Kind as they may be, they don't appear to have the influence we want.

If we try to conjure an image of a woman who is *both* powerful and feminine, chances are we'll draw a blank.

Our inability to marry the masculine and feminine sides of ourselves is due in part to the fact that we don't have a clear picture of what it really means to be a Femininely Empowered Woman, and in the absence of a solid definition, we've confused power with force.

Power Versus Force

Energetically speaking, true power is something that exists at our very core; it's a quiet strength that emanates from within us. When we feel genuinely empowered in a situation, we're relaxed and at ease, open to all possibilities, and content to let others take the lead. We stand in our own authority, certain of our ability to attract the outcomes we desire. Power is a sense of inner certainty that all great leaders possess. Like a radio signal that is clear and strong, the state of genuine empowerment is a potent point of attraction. The universe receives our signal and responds to it instantly and without interference.

Force, on the other hand, is something we throw around to get what we want. It creates an energy field of desperation, anxiety, and turbulence. When we're in this state, our breath becomes shallow, our shoulders tense, and our thoughts scatter in all directions. And while at first glance it's easy to confuse forcefulness with empowerment, we notice the difference in how our actions affect others. When we're in Alpha Bitch mode, we project our harsh, demanding energy onto those around us like a weapon of mass destruction. And no matter how loyal or patient the person on the receiving end of our fury might be, it's almost impossible not to react defensively in the face of such an onslaught. In his breakthrough book, *Power Versus Force: The Hidden Determinants of Human Behavior*, author David R. Hawkins clearly describes the interpersonal dynamics of wielding force:

> Force always creates counter-force; its effect is to polarize rather than unify. Polarization always implies conflict; its cost, therefore, is always high. Because force incites polarization, it inevitably produces a win/lose dichotomy; and because somebody always loses, enemies are always created. Constantly faced with enemies, force requires constant defense. Defensiveness is costly, invariably, whether in the marketplace, politics or international affairs.[1]

Bullies and "mean girls" may appear to have control of a situation, but examine their tactics closely and you'll see that insecurity and fear are driving their tough-girl facade and that their so-called dominance is being held together by force. True power is kind, as well as strong, and does not require a violent display of brashness to prove itself. As Margaret Thatcher so

---

[1] David R. Hawkins M.D., Ph.D., *Power Versus Force: The Hidden Determinants of Human Behavior* (Carlsbad, CA: Hay House, 2002), 133.

eloquently said, "Being powerful is like being a lady. If you have to tell people you are, you aren't."

Now, we're not trying to deny the immediate rush of adrenaline that comes with using aggression and force. Initially, taking control of a situation makes us feel strong and in charge. But trying to sustain a state of authentic power by wielding force is a bit like turning to sugar in hopes of finding lasting energy. It may provide an initial high but eventually we crash. Just as there is no real nutritional value in sugar, there is no lasting satisfaction in plowing over others to get what we want. It may work in the short term, but it takes a lot out of us and also depletes the safety, trust, and personal accountability upon which good relationships are built.

> *Initially, taking control of a situation makes us feel strong and in charge. But trying to sustain a state of authentic power by wielding force is a bit like turning to sugar in hopes of finding lasting energy.*

Wag More, Bark Less

Perhaps you've noticed that charging through life isn't as empowering or as effective as it appears to be. Sure, we may muscle our way through our tasks, but at the end of the day do we find ourselves feeling depleted, anxious, or overwrought? Yes, we may strong-arm others into doing it *our* way, but are our relationships as supportive as we would like them to be? We might justify our abrasiveness by thinking of it as strength—an ability to "get it done"—but if our overbearing methods prevent others from enjoying our company or causes them to flinch at the very sound of our voice, then clearly this aggressive approach is working against us and is less effective than a more feminine one.

The Forceful Alpha in the Workplace

Those of us who have ever worked for someone who talked down to us, insulted or intimidated us, or bossed us around know that these behaviors don't exactly inspire creativity or cooperation. Wielding force at work creates an atmosphere of fear, intimidation, and judgment that absolutely destroys any shred of loyalty or goodwill. Employees and colleagues may start out strong and resilient, but they will get so beaten down that they will only do the minimum expected of them. This is because no matter how hard they try, it is never good enough. Unless there is a culture of mutual respect, they will never feel inspired to bring forth their best work or do the best job possible. They may even secretly talk about their boss behind her back or blatantly go out of their way to sabotage her objectives. One way or another, they'll find a way to revolt.

If, on the other hand, the boss makes it a practice to acknowledge exemplary performances, tasks completed on time, and even good intentions despite less-than-stellar results, others will return her respect and be genuinely motivated to do more for her, not because they are afraid but because they want to. And when she does need to draw attention to a shortcoming, coworkers and employees alike will be more receptive to her feedback because they'll trust her to be fair and respectful in delivering it.

Bitch Tip for Forceful Alphas at Work

Remind yourself that being recognized for your contributions is a basic human need, and rather than playing the role of taskmaster in the office, look for opportunities to extend your appreciation. In most (if not all) cases, the "carrot" will yield much better results than the "stick."

The Forceful Alpha in Relationships

Men who find themselves in an intimate relationship with a Forceful Alpha woman may feel more like a pawn than a partner. Yes, our "take-charge" attitude might have been fun and exciting in the beginning, but if our forcefulness strips him of his individuality or his masculinity, he may start to dislike the person he becomes in our presence. Sexually speaking, most men aren't exactly eager to jump into bed with a tyrant who constantly gives instructions and barks orders. It turns out that they happen to really like their manhood (go figure) and don't enjoy having it shredded to pieces on a regular basis. Our partners will never want to give us the love, attention, and affection we crave as long as we're demanding it from them.

A relationship based on mutual respect and equality simply can't be created through force. Sure, any one of us force-wielding Alpha Females is capable of demanding that our mates pay more attention to us and pick up more around the house. But if we can express our preferences with respect and consideration, we may not only get the house straightened up without asking, but we might just see that old spark in his eyes again. If we come *to* our partners with sensitivity and tact, rather than *at* them with attacks and demands, we might be surprised at how easily we evoke their love and respect. This takes awareness and practice, but the results are well worth the investment. Early in their relationship, Frederick came up with a simple nonconfrontational way to support Christy in making this shift:

> *If we come to our partners with sensitivity and tact, rather than at them with attacks and demands, we might be surprised at how easily we evoke their love and respect.*

> When I first met Frederick, he would refer to me as "Corporate Christy" whenever he felt I was coming across as too forceful or overbearing. It didn't take me long to make the connection that when "Corporate

Christy" was in the house, Frederick would leave the building—if not physically, then emotionally. This little nickname serves as a gentle reminder for me to bring it down a few notches and soften my demeanor. And almost without exception, the moment I am respectful and loving he's instantly attracted—complimenting me, being attentive, and offering his genuine support. The old saying is true: you really *can* catch more flies with honey!

Bitch Tip for the Forceful Partner

Remember that while intimidation and brute force may get him to conform to your wishes, only respect and genuine kindness will inspire him to bring forth his best self.

The Forceful Alpha as a Mother

With our children, wielding force leads to power struggles and causes us to lose our neutrality, our balance, and ultimately, our authority. As parents, we sometimes fear that unless we are rigid and domineering, our kids will walk all over us. In fact, allowing our kids the right to express their points of view doesn't strip us of authority, but earns their love and respect.

Children who are denied the right to express their opinions or their emotions— who are spoken *at* instead of *with*—have a harder time developing a strong sense of self and either return our ag-

> *Allowing our kids the right to express their points of view doesn't strip us of authority, but earns their love and respect.*

gression, feel defeated and withdraw, or flat-out refuse to co-operate simply because they resent our approach. Rebecca, who has raised two wonderful children, a twenty-three-year-old son and a nineteen-year-old daughter, has learned a thing or two about motivating kids while respecting their individuality:

> One thing I know for sure is that *demands always lead to resistance*. I can still hear the distinct sound of my son's heels digging in any time I came at him in Forceful Alpha mode. Even if he agreed in principle with what I was asking, as long as I was raising my voice, threatening, or intimidating him, his developing ego would simply not allow him to give in. But here's what did the trick every time: kindness. In my nicest voice (and yes, at times through gritted teeth) I'd ask, "Hey, could you please pick up your room before dinner? Thanks, I'd appreciate that."

Worked like a charm. And since I wasn't constantly nagging or berating him, when I really did need to flex my parenting muscles, my words had more impact.

Bitch Tip for Forceful Alpha Moms

Remember that a little kindness goes a long way with kids. If you can respectfully *request* of them, rather than *demand* from them, you will invite their cooperation, rather than provoke their resistance. Children learn from example. When you treat them with respect and courtesy, they are much more likely to treat others that way—including you!

The Forceful Alpha as a Friend

Between friends, too much dominating energy can lead to some pretty explosive exchanges. Put two or more Forceful Alphas together in the same room, add a couple of cocktails and even a mildly controversial topic, and they're likely to generate enough drama to rival any reality TV show. While it may be good for network ratings, this combustible mix deprives the Forceful Alpha of the opportunity to forge genuinely supportive and trusting relationships with other women, and drastically limits her choice of friends. Empowered women want nothing to do with someone who is overbearing and aggressive. So, the Forceful Alpha either ends up in the company of meek gals who bend to her will but don't feel safe enough to make a real connection, or she finds herself continually locking horns with other Forceful Alphas. Either way, she misses out on the comfort, camaraderie, and companionship that can only flourish in an environment of equality and respect.

Bitch Tip for Forceful Friends

Practice taking a backseat with your girlfriends once in a while. You don't always have to dominate the conversation or force your advice on them. Share the spotlight by asking a friend about her day and listen without launching into a commentary of your own. Remember, yours are not the only valid opinions, and your views are not necessarily shared by everybody. The more you let others take the lead, the more respected they'll feel and the stronger your bond of friendship will become.

All Bark and No Bite

Whether it shows up at work, in our intimate relationships, or with friends, our hard-as-nails, tough-girl routine is only a facade that we use to hide our insecurities and camouflage our inner doubts. "Get them before they get me" is the motto that drives our brash behaviors. We charge through life, plowing over anyone who gets in our way, not because we feel genuinely empowered but because we believe that using force is the only way we can earn the respect of others or validate our own self-worth. In short:

- We're afraid that if we don't demand respect from others, they will never give it to us.
- We worry that unless we're loud and outspoken, we will never be heard.
- We're afraid that if we back down from an argument, we'll be seen as weak and ineffective.
- We're terrified that if we let our guards down, others will take advantage of us.

These insecurities and self-doubts drive our false bravado and compel us to force our will upon others. We push ourselves relentlessly to do more, be more, and accomplish more in order to prove to ourselves and others that we have value. But unfortunately, even if we manage to master an intimidating bark or construct a convincing persona, it's our *inner* vibration and not our *outer* behavior that magnetizes all experiences into our lives. No matter how well it's concealed, when we're using our will to force things to happen, we're attracting our life experiences, not from confidence and inner strength but from fear and doubt. We then emit energies of mistrust and desperation that repel the very outcomes we are striving to achieve. Fear, urgency, and anxiety are broken, agitated vibrations that grind the creative process to a halt. Anything set into motion from a vibration of pushing or forcing will not yield the results we seek.

We've heard from other authors that when they took on the monumental task of writing a book, they were asked to experience all the necessary lessons to fully master the subject. (You should have seen the claws come out and the fur fly when we were writing our book on female competitiveness!) So as we dove into *Taming Your Alpha Bitch*, we were presented with many opportunities to examine these principles more carefully and to practice our own advice.

On more than one occasion, an inevitable bump in the road would send one or both of us spiraling into Forceful Alpha mode, and we'd find ourselves trying to attack the challenge with brute force. And, of course, each and every time we did, the creative process would come to a grinding halt. Then we'd remind each other to drop the masculine approach and, instead of trying to plow through the task at hand, we'd reconnect with our softer, feminine natures. We'd each take a deep breath and tune in with our inner feminine power, which instantly reconnected us with the unlimited creative energy of the universe.

Without fail, as we owned our certainty in our own creative abilities and the certainty that all the resources we needed were available to us in every moment, the process no longer felt as daunting, and little "signs" would appear to let us know that we were on the right track. Ideas would start to flow, the perfect bit of information would land in our inbox, a friend would call to cheer us on, or a client would share a recent success.

We only resort to force when we forget that we have within us all the resources we need to accomplish what we're setting out to do. Fortunately—as we discovered many times over in the process of writing this book—there is a more direct and efficient way to access all of our creative power, and that is by tapping into its internal, unlimited, universal source.

The Law of Pure Potentiality

The Law of Pure Potentiality is based on the understanding that pure, unbounded consciousness is the very essence of who and what we are and the source of creation itself. Everything we see around us, and every result we are now experiencing, existed first in its potential state; manifestation is pure, unadulterated potentiality expressing itself in physical form.

Take a moment to ponder the implications of this fact. The intelligence that created everything in the universe is a part of us—in fact, it *is* us! Pure Potentiality is the field of all possibilities and the source of all spiritual, emotional, and material wealth. It knows no limits, and when we are internally connected to this essential life energy, we have instant access to all the resources and creativity needed to fulfill any dream. As Deepak Chopra says in his book *The Seven Spiritual Laws of Success*, "When we realize that our true Self is one of pure potentiality, we align with the power that manifests everything in the universe."[2]

2 Deepak Chopra, M.D., *The Seven Spiritual Laws of Success: A Practical Guide to the Fulfillment of Your Dreams* (San Rafael, CA: Amber-Allen Publishing, 1994), 7.

THE FORCEFUL ALPHA 43

When Napoleon Hill, whose work is widely considered the cornerstone of the modern personal growth movement, wrote in his acclaimed book *Think and Grow Rich* that "Whatever the mind of man can conceive and believe, it can achieve," he was describing the immeasurable power of this universal law.

Accessing Pure Potentiality helps restrain our instinct to use force. When we know that we are intimately connected to the resources of a boundless universe, our anxiety dissipates and a sense of ease emerges in the parts of our lives that were once driven by fear. As we align with the Law of Pure Potentiality, we realize that our greatest achievements and successes come to us not through the masculine energies of striving, driving, effort, and force, but through the fluid, magnetic, and feminine qualities of ease and grace.

> *As we align with the Law of Pure Potentiality, we realize that our greatest achievements and successes come to us not through the masculine energies of striving, driving, effort, and force, but through the fluid, magnetic, and feminine qualities of ease and grace.*

Goldie Hawn is a beautiful example of a graceful, feminine woman who is also powerful and wildly successful. An award-winning actress, film director, and producer, her career has spanned five decades and earned her numerous acknowledgments, including an Academy Award and a Golden Globe. Since 1983 she has maintained a thriving relationship with actor Kurt Russell (and we all know that by Hollywood standards, a twenty-five-year relationship is quite an achievement) and she's raised three beautiful, strong, and successful children. When she and Kurt are interviewed together, his love and affection toward her are undeniable. In Hollywood, those who are fortunate enough to work with Goldie have nothing but respect for her and speak only praises. Looking at her life from the outside in, Goldie certainly appears to have it all: she's smart, charming, powerful, and—did we mention—*wildly successful*! We're willing to bet that it was precisely this powerful feminine magnetism that attracted all the love, wealth, and vitality she enjoys. More power to you, Goldie!

When we learn to tap into the wellspring of feminine power that resides within us, we end up producing more inspiring results with more joy and less effort. We still have desire and determination to reach our goals; we know that we can achieve them more effectively by *embodying power* rather than *exerting force*. After all, why should we run on batteries that need constant replacing when we have the ability to plug directly into an unlimited power supply? The chart on the following page illustrates the profound transformation that is possible when we stop wielding force to make things happen and put the Law of Pure Potentiality to work for us instead:

	When Wielding Force	When Embodying Power
How We Perceive Life	• Difficult and tedious • Unfulfilling • Filled with never-ending tasks	• Easy and effortless • Cocreative • Boundless and exciting
How We Perceive Others	• Obstacles to be overcome • Intimidating and threatening • Inferior and exhausting	• Respectful • Kind • Resourceful and trustworthy
How Others Perceive Us	• Insensitive • Aggressive and abrasive • Critical and demeaning • Mean-spirited • Intolerant and demanding	• Empowered and approachable • Elegant and graceful • Centered • Magnetic • Confident
How We Feel	• Pressured and stressed • Frustrated • Agitated • Out of balance • Overwhelmed	• Empowered and creative • Connected • Relaxed • Focused • Certain, strong, and secure

Inner Connection—The Key That Activates the Law of Pure Potentiality

So, how can we easily fulfill our desires by activating the Law of Pure Potentiality? We first have to realize that once we've identified something we want—whether it's a new job, a husband, a higher salary, or simply a more joy-filled lifestyle—we have two basic choices to attract what we want. We can take the masculine approach and use force to hunt down and trap whatever it is we're seeking or call upon our feminine power and the unbounded energy of Pure Potentiality by aligning our vibrations with the outcomes we desire. From this feminine approach we turn inward, using *energy*, not *effort*, to magnetically draw to us what we desire. Now this method may seem somewhat passive and less effective than a masculine, outwardly focused one, but why work hard and struggle when you don't have to? It is precisely this effortless feminine approach that wise women like Goldie Hawn employ to create their phenomenal lives.

> *To attract what we want . . . we can call upon our feminine power and the unbounded energy of Pure Potentiality by aligning our vibrations with the outcomes we desire.*

Establishing a strong inner connection is the fastest way to align our individual energies with the greater intelligence of the universe. The stronger the connection we forge with our inner self and the more trust we put in ourselves, the less we feel the need to throw our weight around. When we know deep within that flowing through us is the power that creates worlds, we see how ludicrous it is to waste our precious energy trying to force things to happen. As we learn to access and experience the power of these higher levels of consciousness, we realize that we are not isolated individuals who have to fight tooth and nail for a few scraps; we are daughters of an abundant universe in which all things are possible, and the realities we desire are ours for the making. While the Alpha Bitch approach to life is calculated and intense, the Femininely Empowered Woman approach is magnetic and graceful.

> *While the Alpha Bitch approach to life is calculated and intense, the Femininely Empowered Woman approach is magnetic and graceful.*

The feminine approach is inwardly centered, being-oriented, collaborative, and cocreative, while the masculine tactic is action-oriented, externally focused, and domineering. The masculine approach requires a great deal of physical, mental, and emotional effort, while the feminine path enables us to accomplish more with less exertion. Remember, it's the coherence of our energy, not necessarily the degree of our efforts, that determines our end results. The masculine way leaves us feeling aggressive, short-tempered, and on edge; embodying the feminine reduces the turbulence in our lives and allows us to maintain a sense of grace and fluidity, even when things don't go as planned. Spiritual teacher and acclaimed author Eckhart Tolle states, "You find peace not by rearranging the circumstances of your life, but by realizing who you are at the deepest level."[3] There is but

---

[3] Eckhart Tolle, *Stillness Speaks* (Novato, CA: New World Library, 2003), 64.

one road that leads to this life-altering realization, and we can only find it by turning our attention within.

Remember, it's the coherence of our energy, not necessarily the degree of our efforts, that determines our end results.

By withdrawing our attention from the outer world of possessions and attainments and grounding ourselves in our own inner core of power, our vibration shifts from desperate and intense to clear, calm, and focused. Here are some practical suggestions for making this shift:

- Set aside time each day to be alone without interruption (journaling is a great practice to do during this time).
- Take a walk outside. The peace and beauty of your surroundings will promote an inner connection.
- Meditate—just a few minutes a day of quieting your mind can be deeply revitalizing and connects you to the nonphysical realm.
- Listen to the guided meditation we've created at www.tamingyouralphabitch.com that leads you on an inward journey to connect with your intuition and the field of Pure Potentiality.

In addition to feeling calmer and more at ease, turning inward connects us to our intuition. We join with the part of us that is wise and all-knowing, the part that is one with the greater intelligence of life. We're able to head off potential upsets or detours because we instinctively sense which actions will lead us more directly to the outcomes we desire. We call this taking *inspired action*, by heeding the guidance that comes from our inner wisdom rather than our egos. From this inner base of security, we become better parents, partners, lovers, and friends. We emit a vibration of inner calm that is felt by everything and everyone. Instead of working alone and toiling to create the results we want, we begin to collaborate with the universe to cocreate a miraculous life. Establishing a firm inner connection introduces a new rhythm to our lives that allows things to fall into place naturally, easily, and in perfect timing. When we're internally connected to the field of limitless possibilities, magic begins to happen.

> *"Mastering others is strength. Mastering yourself*
> *is true power."*
> —LAO TZU

The following exercise will help to identify beliefs that keep you from embracing your most authentic, powerful, and essential self.

EXERCISE
From Wielding Force to Embodying Power

Set aside twenty to thirty minutes of uninterrupted time to complete this exercise, making sure that you have a journal or a piece of paper and pen nearby to record any insights or actions that may arise.

To begin, allow yourself to recall a recent experience when you actually caught yourself in the act of wielding force. It might have been at work, with friends or family members, or in your relationship with your husband or children. See if you can replay it as if it were happening in this moment. As vividly as you can, picture the people involved in the situation and the circumstances that led up to it. What were you saying or doing? How were they responding to you? Be as honest with yourself as you can and write down whatever details you can recall.

Identify what you were feeling in that moment. Give yourself permission to be vulnerable and to feel the underlying fears, doubts, and insecurities that triggered your forceful behavior. Ask yourself, "What was I afraid would happen if I wasn't in charge or acting aggressively?" and allow yourself to hear whatever answers arise. Allow yourself to feel how ultimately *dis*empowering force and aggression are.

Now, listen to the thoughts that led to the emotions you are feeling. Give yourself time to really listen. Write down as many thoughts as you can without judging them.

Allow yourself to go behind your thoughts to the core belief that ignited these thoughts. Be patient, simply letting the belief reveal itself in perfect time. How do you feel when you hold this belief in your awareness? Does it make you feel small and weak, scared or vulnerable? Describe your experience as you uncover the limiting belief.

Ask yourself what new belief you could hold that would make you feel more self-assured and empowered. What statements could you affirm that would lead to more empowering behaviors? Try these out and see how they feel:

* *I have all the power and creativity I need to make my dreams a reality.*
* *I attain my heart's desires through ease and grace. My strength comes from within me.*
* *I am part of a powerful and abundant universe.*

Write down your new belief in your journal and allow it to become deeply anchored in your consciousness by saying it aloud several times. Allow yourself to fully embody the meaning of this new statement. Even if you don't fully believe it at first, over time it will become your predominant way of thinking.

Ask yourself what actions you could take—right now or in the future—to align your behaviors with this new belief statement. Write down whatever ideas come to you. Allow yourself to feel the way you would feel if you actually took those actions. Would you be more self-assured and empowered? More centered and relaxed?

With your next breath, consciously and deliberately release any thoughts or feelings of force, and allow yourself to feel empowered as you state your new belief. Make a commitment to repeat this empowering belief often, each time feeling the truth of the statement. Take a few moments to savor this feeling.

• • • • • • • • • • • • • •

Go to www.alphabitchbook.com to download an additional "Embodying Power" meditation, and use the authorization code TYABFREE.

Bitch Tip

When you catch yourself trying to dominate others through force, remember that your true power comes from within. Reestablish an inner connection with that unlimited source, and that which you've been trying to obtain will be magnetized to you naturally.

chapter two
The Controlling Alpha

The Controlling Alpha female is easy to spot. She's the one heading up the Neighborhood Watch program, running the PTA meetings, and planning the itinerary for her child's field trip two months in advance. If she's going out for the evening, she not only chooses the restaurant and insists upon a particular table but probably also "suggests" the most appropriate seating arrangements for everyone in her party. We'll find her in grocery store aisles, dispensing advice to complete strangers about which products to buy, or recognize her by observing her family: they're the ones obediently trailing behind her as she charges through the mall. She's also the friend we call before making an important purchase or choosing a vacation destination. She is a woman who is in the know and someone to whom others regularly turn to for guidance.

In fact, the Controlling Alpha is often incredibly capable and resourceful. She's the woman we want by our side if our ship is going down because she'll know where to find the life vests and exactly how far to inflate them for maximum buoyancy! She expects the best from herself and others, and

although she can get annoying and even downright condescending at times, we can usually count on her to get the job
done right and in record time.

The Controlling Alpha might be relentlessly outspoken,
arguing for her position until those around her finally cave,
or she may take a more subtle approach. A quick, disap-
proving glance or a caustic one-liner delivered at just the
right moment leaves no room
for doubt in the mind of the
receiver that the Controlling
Alpha knows best. When
people don't get the mes-
sage—or worse, if they refuse to heed her advice—she
becomes even more controlling and manipulative. She
is convinced that her way is
the right way (and, let's be
honest, the *only* way) to do
things. Whether she comes
off like a demanding drill sergeant or prefers to pull the
strings quietly from behind the scenes, the Controlling
Alpha knows that over time her tenacity will pay off, and
eventually her friends, family members, kids, and coworkers will end up doing exactly what she wants.

At work, the Controlling Alpha definitely knows how to
make things happen and she's usually not shy about voicing
her opinions—solicited or not. She is a natural leader who
is unafraid to take charge, especially in a crisis. She'll be the
first to admit that her workload is too heavy, yet her lack of

> *A quick, disapproving
> glance or a caustic one-liner
> delivered at just the right
> moment leaves no room for
> doubt in the mind of the
> receiver that the Controlling
> Alpha knows best.*

faith in her colleagues' abilities makes it extremely difficult for her to delegate. When she must work in tandem with a team of people, she finds it almost impossible to keep from micromanaging every move. In her professional pursuits, she is usually exceptionally ambitious and hardworking and may even consider herself indispensable. But she fails to realize how her overbearing approach ends up alienating her from superiors and subordinates.

In her intimate relationships, you can be sure the Controlling Alpha is the one running the show. She sets the agenda and dictates not only what the couple will do but also when, how, and with whom. For her many talents, negotiating and compromising are foreign concepts to her. Oh sure, she may ask for her partner's opinion, but she'll eventually shoot it down if it contradicts her own. Before long she's controlling his wardrobe, his dinner entrées, his weekend pastimes, and even what he does while he is out with his friends. Through her actions and her attitudes, the Controlling Alpha sends a very clear message to her mate: "You are incompetent and untrustworthy; therefore, I must take control." Of course, this doesn't exactly make for a mutually satisfying partnership; she treats the man in her life like one of her kids and then complains that he acts like a child.

As a mother, the Controlling Alpha is the quintessential "helicopter parent," hell-bent on hovering over and managing every aspect of her children's behaviors. One way or another, she will make sure they toe the line—either by ceaselessly barking orders, or by playing the martyr and shouting things like, "I was in labor for forty-eight hours without painkillers; the least you could do is pick up your socks." And while she knows exactly which buttons to push to elicit the desired responses from her kids, she misses the larger opportunity to support her children to grow into strong, resourceful, and independent adults.

In her friendships, the Controlling Alpha is the one in charge. She's the one directing her girlfriends' lives, from where they'll be lunching to whom they should be dating. And she fully expects (and even insists) that they follow her guidance, even when they never asked for her advice. She's the friend who plans our social calendars, helps organize our closets, and directs us on what to wear, eat, and read. Although she genuinely cares about her girlfriends' well-being, she can be *overly* invested in their lives. Consequently, she can't understand why they pull away from her or get snippy with her.

To put it bluntly, Controlling Alpha Bitches are difficult to work with, to live with, and, well, to *be* with!

A classic Controlling Alpha is Miranda Hobbes, the lawyer on the television series *Sex and the City*. Her friends Carrie, Charlotte, and Samantha put up with her rigid, bossy manner, even though she can be a bit much to tolerate at times. Miranda is very outspoken and is always quick to give her opinions. Her husband, Steve, is no stranger to her controlling ways, either. In fact, Miranda even had a hard time relaxing and letting go on their honeymoon. She was so anxious about being out of her element—away from her work, computer, and controlled environment—that she could not allow herself to just enjoy the time with her husband. In another episode, Charlotte wanted to throw her a baby shower. Miranda begrudgingly agreed, but only on her terms: "Okay, but no cutsie, storkie s--t. Just an adult, dignified lunch with presents, which I will open after everyone leaves. No games, no crustless bread. I want fried chicken." Charlotte agreed to all of her conditions—she was afraid not to. Later in the series we see an explosive fight between friends, when Miranda states her opinion about Carrie's choice to move to France with a new boyfriend. Although Miranda is very successful in her career, her rigidity and control prevent her from fully enjoying her exciting lifestyle, her great friends, and her wonderful husband and child.

The Woman in the Mirror

Chances are good that there are at least a few Controlling Alphas in your life—you might even count yourself among them. Breathe easy, girls, because you're among friends. Let's face it, when we're in Controlling Alpha mode, we are compelled to direct just about everything and everyone. We, just like Miranda, have to put in our two cents regarding all decisions, big or small, whether they involve us or not. No doubt we've been told by friends and even strangers that we're too controlling, and most of us would be the first to agree.

Just in case you're wondering where you rank, take the following quiz:

THE CONTROLLER—ARE YOU THIS TYPE OF ALPHA BITCH?

1. *If a friend threw you a surprise party, you would most likely react ...*

   A Surprised! And pleasantly so.
   B Taken aback at first, but eventually able to roll with it.
   C Annoyed or even offended—you'll decide how and with whom to celebrate your birthday, thank you very much!
   D A surprise party? Please. Not even your closest friend could pull that over on you!

2. *When assigned to work on a group project, you ...*

   A Present your ideas but don't force them on others.
   B Go along with the majority vote even though you're sure your way is the right way.
   C Say you're fine with others taking the lead, but feel extremely anxious when you're not in charge.
   D Nominate yourself as the project manager, even if it ruffles a few feathers. After all, there's work to get done!

3. *If you found out that your spouse intends to vote for the presidential candidate you aren't backing, you would ...*

   A Do your best to understand your differing political views.
   B Accept his choice, even if you don't agree with it.
   C Itemize all the reasons why he's making the wrong decision.
   D Continue badgering him until he changes his mind and votes with you (or tells you he is, at least).

4. *After delegating a task to a coworker, you notice that her approach is completely different than one you would take. You ...*

   A Don't mind how she does it as long as she gets good results.
   B Wish you'd been more specific up front about how *you* wanted the project to be done.

C   Keep close tabs on things to make sure she stays on point, and
end up investing more time than if you'd done it yourself.
D   Take the project back. Who needs the aggravation!

5. *When someone other than you is driving, you . . .*

A   Relax and enjoy the scenery.
B   Hold your tongue, but wear a hole in the carpet from pressing
on the imaginary brake.
C   "Help" the driver by offering suggestions about the best lane to
choose and route to take.
D   You avoid being a passenger whenever possible.

6. *If your significant other walks in wearing what you consider to be a
less-than-coordinated outfit, you . . .*

A   Casually mention that he might consider a more stylish look.
B   Appreciate his somewhat vanguard sense of style.
C   Give him "the look" and make him change his attire.
D   That would never happen; you lay out all his clothes ahead of
time.

7. *When you and your spouse need to make a major purchase, you . . .*

A   Talk it over and arrive at a mutual decision.
B   Double-check his research because you know he can't be trusted
on his own.
C   Do your own research so that you can present a compelling case
for why you've found the perfect style or brand.
D   Make the purchase yourself and then give him your reasons.

8. *How easy is it for you to admit when you're wrong?*

A   Not a problem.
B   It depends on the situation.
C   Extremely difficult.
D   Extremely easy because you're never wrong!

continued on next page . . .

continued...

9. *When you see your child doing a household chore at a rate far slower than you could do it yourself, you ...*

A   Offer to lend a hand, but allow time for the learning process to unfold.
B   Become anxious or irritated.
C   Practically have to sit on your hands to keep from taking over.
D   Jump in and complete the task the "right way"!

10. *If you knew in advance that you would be laid up for a while after surgery, you'd be more likely to ...*

A   Trust that your loved ones will come through for you; after all, what are friends for?
B   Assign each family member a particular set of tasks so you're sure everything will be handled.
C   Stay in the hospital as long as possible because you're guaranteed to get your needs met while you're there.
D   Hire an around-the-clock nurse to care for you so you won't have to worry about others letting you down.

SCORING KEY:

1. a-1, b-3, c-5, d-4 • 2. a-1, b-3, c-4, d-5 • 3. a-2, b-1, c-4, d-5 • 4. a-1, b-3, c-4, d-5 • 5. a-1, b-4, c-3, d-5 6. a-2, b-1, c-4, d-5 • 7. a-1, b-3, c-4, d-5 • 8. a-1, b-2, c-4, d-5 • 9. a-2, b-4, c-3, d-5 • 10. a-1, b-3, c-4, d-5

ASSESSMENT:

Using the number that corresponds to each answer you gave, add up your total number of points.

If you scored 20 or fewer points, take a deep breath because you are not a Controlling Alpha.

If you scored between 21 and 35 points, you probably worry that letting go of control will lead to chaos—something you try to avoid at all costs—and feel annoyed, restless, or agitated anytime someone other than you is calling the shots.

If you scored between 35 and 50 points, it's highly likely that your controlling behavior is seriously undermining your relationships, your enjoyment of life, and your peace of mind. Read on to discover how embracing a mindset of allowing can take you farther and faster toward fulfillment than controlling ever did, and with much less effort and far greater joy.

Intellectually at least, we know that our interfering ways often hinder us more than they help. Pushing and prodding others only makes them dig their heels in deeper and resist the very things we're trying to get them to do. It's also safe to say that most of us Controlling Alphas have tried, on at least a few occasions, to tame our more forceful urges. Through gritted teeth we've smiled in the face of our anxieties and made ourselves utter a casual, "Whatever."

But no matter how many times our inner control freak has been bound, gagged, and hog-tied, it always returns with a vengeance. Why? Because control is a strategy we've developed to avoid our more vulnerable feelings. The fact is, most of us become incredibly anxious, restless, or agitated anytime we're not calling the shots.

While to the outside world we may project an image of competency and authority, beneath this facade is fear and insecurity. We resort to control, not because we're ultraconfident in our own abilities but because deep down we don't trust others to come through for us. We are afraid.

- We're nervous that if we don't oversee our spouse's every move, they will end up hurting, disappointing, or betraying us.
- We're secretly terrified that something will happen to our children if we fail to manage every aspect of their lives.
- We fear that unless we anticipate every possible misstep at work, we'll experience judgment, failure, or outright humiliation.

Control is a strategy we've developed to avoid our more vulnerable feelings. The fact is, most of us become incredibly anxious, restless, or agitated anytime we're not calling the shots. We resort to control, not because we're ultraconfident in our own abilities but because deep down we don't trust others to come through for us.

But it's not just others we mistrust. Our lack of confidence in others reflects a basic mistrust in ourselves, as well as an inability to have faith in life as a whole.

Now at this point you're probably thinking, "Of course I trust myself; that's why I do everything *myself!*" But actually, we only resort to outward control when inside we doubt our capacity to handle the scary, painful, sad, or unexpected situations that life could throw our way. Control is the crutch we lean on to give us a sense of security. If only we could manage every last detail, we tell ourselves, we could avoid the pain of the unknown, eliminate the element of surprise, and sidestep the potential disasters that lie in our path. As long as we are in control, at least we know what to expect.

We only resort to outward control when inside we doubt our capacity to handle the scary, painful, sad, or unexpected situations that life could throw our way. Control is the crutch we lean on to give us a sense of security.

Our attempts at control may seem to be motivated by confidence, but they actually expose an underlying belief that things won't work out for us unless they are kept under our constant supervision. This lack of faith is at the root of our control issues, and to resolve them we must find our way back to our natural, trusting state. In the same way that deepening the connection to our inner, essential selves and the universe softened our Forceful Alpha tendencies, returning to our natural and trusting self relinquishes our controlling stronghold.

When we are born, we are in a complete and absolute state of trust. We trust that our parents will care for us, that our surroundings will support us, and ultimately, that life will provide for us. But fast-forward a few chapters in the life story of nearly every Controlling Alpha, and we'll inevitably find some initial incident—or a sequence of them—that eroded our original faith in life.

During development, if this essential trust foundation is shattered, it's easy to see why some turn to control as a way to build a sense of security. If, for example, we grew up in a dangerous or chaotic environment or perceived our caretakers as incapable of protecting us, exercising our control muscles was probably an excellent coping strategy that helped us to defend against any further loss or trauma. Overseeing every last detail enabled us to better predict the outcome of vulnerable situations.

If we're honest, most of us will readily admit that our controlling nature actually undermines our peace of mind, our enjoyment of life, and our ability to create all that we desire.

But if we keep fast-forwarding twenty, thirty, or forty years later and find that this mindset is still firmly in place, we now have to ask ourselves to what extent, if any, does it serve us? If we're honest, most of us will readily admit that our controlling nature actually undermines our peace of mind, our enjoyment of life, and our ability to create all that we desire.

The Cost of Control: Is It Worth It?

Control comes at a pretty steep price. Sure, we may feel important because we're the ones everyone looks to for guidance, but how often do we find ourselves feeling exhausted, undernourished, and stressed out from trying to hold it all together? Yes, we may succeed in getting others to do exactly as we want, but are they doing it because they want to or because they feel coerced? We may take pride in how our well-ordered lives run, but if our micromanaging nature causes us to constantly work at keeping our lives running perfectly, we never relax and enjoy the fruits of our labor. Clearly the coping mechanism that once helped us to survive is now blocking our ability to benefit from the freedom, joy, and fulfillment we seek.

Maybe you've noticed that the harder you try to control others, the faster you drive them away. Yep, it turns out being micromanaged and constantly corrected is actually not all that enjoyable! If you've ever experienced the scrutiny of a Controlling Alpha Bitch, you know this firsthand. No self-respecting person will tolerate being under someone's thumb for long. Husbands, coworkers, and kids eventually tire of being nagged, nitpicked, and told what to do. And the more you try to ensure your own happiness by directing their every move, the less genuinely motivated they are to please you.

The Controlling Alpha in the Workplace

It's natural to want to flex our control muscles at work. After all, most jobs require us to take charge, oversee projects, and even manage others. And because these expectations are in place, it's easy to understand how we can fall into the trap of becoming a Controlling Alpha in the workplace. Perhaps you've had the pleasure of being under

> ## Bitch Tips for Managing
> ## Control in the Workplace
>
> • Wait to be asked before offering input.
> • When giving colleagues suggestions or constructive
>   feedback, begin by pointing out something they're do-
>   ing well, and be skillful and sensitive in your critique.
> • When presented with ideas or methods that are differ-
>   ent than yours, pause before immediately disregard-
>   ing them; remember that your opinion is not the only
>   one or necessarily the right one. Be open to your co-
>   workers' ideas.

the thumb of a micromanaging, opinion-giving colleague
or boss who's constantly looking over your shoulder, criti-
cizing your work, or questioning your every decision. You
can't be yourself under her watchful eye; just knowing that
she's near makes you extremely anxious, or you second-
guess yourself. Working for—or with—a Controlling Alpha
is enough to squeeze the creative juices right out of you.

When our inner Controlling Alpha comes out, not
only are we no fun to be around but we also create para-
noia and unnecessary pressure in the workplace. Sometimes the only respite for our coworkers is the comfort
of a private bathroom stall, far away from us. They find
any excuse to get out of the office and away from our intense scrutiny. We need to understand that our controlling
ways stifle, rather than inspire, creativity. Evoking fear and

doubt in our colleagues is the surest way to shut down the creative genius in them. Even though our goal is to get the job done well, by interfering and critiquing, we slow down productivity and create resistance in our office mates.

The Controlling Alpha as a Partner

In our intimate relationships, when disdain and resentment takes root in the space where admiration and affection used to grow, unpleasant outcomes lurk around the corner. The spouse of an unrelenting Controlling Alpha may simply leave her to find a woman who allows him the right to exercise his opinions. And if he does choose to stay in the relationship, chances are good that he'll find other ways to "leave."

An overwhelming number of women that we meet in our practices and workshops complain that their mates are "checked out"; that is, they no longer participate in their marriage or contribute to the household, and she ends up bearing the brunt of responsibility all by herself. This occurs when the partner of a Controlling Alpha concludes that challenging her will only lead to tension or provoke a full-blown fight so he opts for compliance and passivity instead. Over time, he loses more and more power in the relationship until he simply fades into the background. He stops trying to make decisions; in essence, he stops "showing up" for his mate, which only further reinforces her perception that he needs to be managed. Notice the vicious cycle?

Despite how passive he may appear, you can be sure that a man whose opinions are continually disregarded accumulates a lot of resentment over time. He may not express his anger outwardly, but he'll find a way to reclaim some power. You know the deal: he arrives home late the night you're hosting a dinner party with friends, he turns his cell phone off so you can't get in touch with him, or he forgets to pick up the dry cleaning the night before your big presentation at work. Of course, his passive-aggressive behavior only leaves us feeling more out of control, so we pull the reins even tighter. Our inability to tolerate anyone who doesn't see things exactly as we do can end up destroying the trust and intimacy in the relationships we cherish the most.

Bitch Tips for the Controlling Partner

- Ask him to tell you when he's feeling controlled or pressured by you.
- Set daily goals for yourself, such as, "Today I won't check my husband's Facebook page, make him a list of things to do, or question his whereabouts when he gets home."
- Find a trusted friend to talk to when you're tempted to launch into controlling behaviors.
- Redirect your attention to your own needs—take a bath, enjoy a cup of tea, read a chapter of your favorite book, or take a long walk.
- Reward yourself when you recognize a controlling behavior and choose not to give into it.

The Controlling Alpha as a Mother

If there is one area of life where our "My way or the highway" attitude will most certainly lead us straight off the proverbial cliff, it's with our children. When they're little, our kids are dependent upon us, and monitoring them is necessary. But as they get older, they outgrow our direction and need us to loosen the reins. To make the shift from "smother mother" to empowering parent, we must understand that our real job is not to manage our children but to help them build a solid foundation that will empower them to manage themselves.

Of course, it's only natural to want to shield our children from all of life's evils and protect them from experiencing undue pain; the instinct to keep them safe is literally hardwired into our DNA. But when we insist on doing for them what they should be doing for themselves, we cross the fine line between helping our kids and disabling them. If we tie their shoes every morning to ensure they never trip and skin a knee, how will they ever learn this basic skill? If we're always reminding them to eat their lunch, do their homework, and put their toys away, they learn to rely on us instead of themselves, and we stunt their ability to be independent adults. We may keep them

> *To make the shift from "smother mother" to empowering parent, we must understand that our real job is not to manage our children but to help them build a solid foundation that will empower them to manage themselves.*

from ever feeling the sting of a stolen bike, a poor grade, or an empty stomach, but in the process, we also prevent them from discovering their own resources and rob them of important life lessons. When they grow up, they are virtually lost without mommy directing them.

Perhaps you've heard the story of a man who discovered a butterfly struggling to emerge from its cocoon. Thinking he was being helpful, he carefully tore open the covering and eased the little butterfly out as gently as he could. But to his dismay, the tiny creature's wings were shriveled and useless. When butterflies first emerge, they go through an intense struggle to break the cocoon. This battle is nature's way of forcing blood flow into the wings. Unless this process unfolds without interruption, the butterfly never becomes strong enough to support itself once it finally reaches freedom.

Likewise, we have to give our children the opportunity to struggle, to make mistakes, and to learn from them. They're proud of the way they negotiated half of a sandwich from a friend the day they forgot their lunch, how they borrowed a spare pencil from a classmate right before the test, or persuaded a teacher to give them an extension on a missed assignment. These are life skills that every successful adult needs, skills that will never be developed if our interference deprives them of the opportunity to correct their mistakes.

When our efforts to guide our kids escalate into controlling them, we keep them from reaching developmental milestones. Stepping in to lend a helping hand becomes overstepping their boundaries, protecting becomes suffocating, and mothering becomes smothering.

If we are Controlling Alphas, we run the risk of fostering a sense of helplessness in our kids, inadvertently sending the message that we don't trust them to make good choices on their own. If we jump in with our own solutions the moment they start contemplating the best way to handle a problem, we're unwittingly instilling a lack of trust in them. Like the story of the man and the butterfly, we end up crippling the people that we love the most.

When our efforts to guide our kids escalate into controlling them, we keep them from reaching developmental milestones. Stepping in to lend a helping hand becomes overstepping their boundaries, protecting becomes suffocating, and mothering becomes smothering.

So, how do we know when to jump in and when to step aside with our kids? Just ask them! Even the youngest children—babies included—can communicate their needs and let us know when to back off! Not too long ago Christy was lavishing her one-month-old son, Alex, with kisses all over his face and neck. (Who can blame her, he's so kissable!) As she was going in for another round of smooches to his pudgy cheeks, he blocked her attempt by putting up both hands. He seemed to be saying, "Enough already, *smother mother!*" Thankfully, Christy listened to what Alex was telling her and respected his space.

Before assuming they want our help tying their shoes or our expertise filling out their college application, ask how we can best support them. Of course, there may be times when they veer off path and need us to take charge; for example, if they're getting involved with a dangerous crowd of friends, battling an addiction or depression, or exhibiting irresponsible sexual behaviors. Then it's absolutely appropriate and necessary to step in and take over for our kids, until they prove that they can once again manage themselves.

Every parent is aware that the important job of parenting never came with an operation manual. It's also true that we must take into account each new situation and the unique disposition of every child. As parents we feel our way through each passing stage of our child's development, correcting along the way. A general rule of thumb, however, is that the older our children get, the less input we should have in their lives. Our kids can indicate if we are controlling or allowing. Some things to look for:

- Do they seem generally happy and content?
- Are they open and excited to be around us?
- Are they self-sufficient and self-motivated?
- Do they seem confident and willing to try new things?

You can also use your own feelings as indicators as to whether the Controlling Alpha within has taken over:

- Do you feel burdened, stressed, or resentful around your kids?
- Are you terrified when they're away from you?

- Do you get angry when they want to make their own choices and refuse to listen to your "suggestions"?

Our kids don't need us playing quarterback, designing every play and directing their every move. We serve them better as cheerleaders who applaud their successes, remain on the sidelines, and give them the freedom to play their own game. When our children present us with a problem, our first instincts may be to immediately offer the "best" solution. A better response is to let them come up with their own solutions. This shows we trust them to make good choices. Once they come up with ideas, we can elaborate or offer suggestions, while still validating their ideas by affirming them in some way. But then leave the final decision up to them so they can start to trust themselves and their decision-making abilities. As a parent, offering suggestions and guidance is all we can do—providing tools to help a child build a successful path is the best gift. Remember, our job as moms is not to do for them but to *empower* them to do for themselves.

Remember, our job as moms is not to do for them but to empower *them to do for themselves.*

Bitch Tips for Controlling Moms

- When you find it hard to watch your kids struggle on their own, seek support from a spouse, fellow mother, or trusted friend.
- Ask yourself, "What am I afraid will happen if I'm not overseeing this situation?" Often just identifying the fear can diminish its hold on you.
- Reassure yourself that no matter what happens, you are capable of handling it. This gives you the opportunity to validate your strength and resourcefulness.
- When your kids share a problem with you, resist the urge to solve it for them. Instead, just listen or ask them how they might handle it.
- Keep a mental list of the many ways your children have already successfully navigated life's challenges. This will help to soothe your fears that without you they will fall apart, and it may help you see them as competent and capable.

The Controlling Alpha as a Friend

Nobody likes to be told what to do or how to do it. Whether we're two or forty-two, having our ideas, choices, methods, or style judged is simply not enjoyable. When we feel it's our right to "improve" our friends, or claim to know what's

best for them, we cross the line from being interested in
their lives to *interfering* with their lives. We hear women
complain how often new
friendships start out hopeful and fun but somehow
fizzle out over time. They
don't understand why other
women pull away from them
or stop returning their calls.
(Of course, when we suggest
that control may be at play,
they're usually quick to disagree and tell us what they
think it must be!) *Hmmm.*

*When we feel it's our right to
"improve" our friends, or claim
to know what's best for them,
we cross the line from being
interested in their lives to
interfering with their lives.*

   Few will put up with being scrutinized and criticized.
She will tire of our "subtle" attempts at changing her:
"Oh, you're going to wear that tonight? Are you still dating what's-his-name? You're ordering pizza? I thought you
wanted to lose weight?" We have to realize that in correcting
our friend's choices and judging her life decisions, we are in
essence questioning her wisdom. She may start to feel like
we think she's not capable of picking out an appropriate
outfit, selecting a good mate, or making a smart meal choice
without our guidance. Feeling belittled and disempowered
in our presence will send her searching for a friend who
builds her up rather than tear her down. Of course, she may
try to speak up and let us know that our interfering ways
are bothering her, but if this goes unheeded she'll eventually move on, leaving us wondering why nobody appreci-
ates our good advice.

Bitch Tips for the Controlling Friend

- Redirect the attention (and energy) you place on your friends back on yourself.
- Before offering your opinion, take a deep breath and ask yourself whether this advice will empower her or disempower her.
- Share your desire to change your controlling patterns with her. Ask her to point out when she's feeling pressured to comply with you.
- Challenge yourself to learn something from the differences between you and allow your friendship to open your mind to new possibilities.
- Use your differences as an opportunity to strengthen your individual choices. Perhaps watching a friend go down a certain path will solidify your decision to take a different route.

Forcing our will upon our children, partners, coworkers, and friends is not only detrimental to these relationships but also takes a toll on us, both physically and emotionally. When we're in Controlling Alpha mode it's as though we have blinders on. We literally can't see how much energy it takes to live in a state of near-perpetual vigilance. Because we're so reluctant to let others take the lead, we end up shouldering many of life's burdens alone, then feel overwhelmed because no one else seems to be pitching in to help. In other words, we insist on calling all the shots and resent when others relinquish responsibility to us! No wonder life stops being fun and exciting and starts to feel like martyrdom.

Have you ever hosted a party and become so obsessed with attending to every little detail that you couldn't enjoy yourself? Or worse, you couldn't wait for the night to end? Trying to control a situation is probably the fastest way to guarantee our own misery because control eats away the pleasures of spontaneity and replaces them with worry, anxiety, and resistance.

The Law of Allowing

Control restricts the stream of abundance that is always flowing to us. Imagine trying to water a garden with a hose that has a kink in it. The garden doesn't flourish, and it's not because there is a lack of water, but because the needed nourishment is temporarily cut off.

Control is the proverbial kink in the hose that keeps us from receiving all that life has to offer. To put it simply, clenched fists can't receive gifts. But if we can learn to relax and allow things to unfold as they are—if we loosen our grip—we'll be better able to greet the unanticipated with eagerness and enthusiasm. Instead of thinking of ourselves as directors who

> *Control is the proverbial kink in the hose that keeps us from receiving all that life has to offer. To put it simply, clenched fists can't receive gifts.*

must orchestrate every detail to make sure it all falls into place, we can view ourselves as the instruments through which good things flow.

This subtle shift in perception is at the core of how the Law of Allowing is activated. When we put forth little resistance and allow positive energy to flow easily to and through us, we move from controlling to allowing. From this accepting mindset, we are open to receive that for which we've asked. As we learn to surrender our need for control, we release resistance and *allow* abundance, freedom, and joy to flow in and out of our lives without restriction. Activating the Law of Allowing requires us to admit that our opinions, ideas, and agendas are not as all-powerful as we may believe. Rather than seizing control in a situation, we place our faith in a force greater than ourselves to coordinate the events of our lives. Instead of feeling that we alone must work to fulfill our dreams, we can sit back and watch the magic unfold with the help of the universe. And what a relief it is to discover that we no longer have to go it alone!

When we try to control everything, we lose sight of the fact that there is a greater intelligence at play—a force that is infinitely more capable than we are at orchestrating the way our lives unfold, from the most mundane details to our most cherished aspirations. If we ever doubt this fact, all we need to do is look at the natural world and we'll find ample evidence of an intelligent hand at work. Deepak Chopra writes in *The Seven Spiritual Laws of Success*:

> If you observe nature at work, you will
> see that...grass doesn't try to grow, it just

Barnes & Noble Booksellers #2735
1212 Greenbrier Pkwy
Chesapeake, VA 23320
757-382-0220

STR:2735 REG:005 TRN:7655 CSHR:Angie

Green Tea
    9781575662435   T1
    (1 @ 5.99)   5.99
Taming Your Alpha Bitch: How to Be Fierc
    9781936661152   T1
    (1 @ 14.95)   14.95

Subtotal   20.94
Sales Tax T1 (6.000%)   1.26
TOTAL   22.20
VISA   20
    Card#: XXXXXXXXXXXXX4256
    Expdate: XX/XX
    Auth: 730792
    Entry Method: Swiped

A MEMBER WOULD HAVE SAVED   2.10

Thanks for shopping at
Barnes & Noble

101.31A   07/09/2013 08:06PM

CUSTOMER COPY

exceptions:

A store credit for the purchase price will be issued (i) for purchases made by check less than 7 days prior to the date of return, (ii) when a gift receipt is presented within 60 days of purchase, (iii) for textbooks, or (iv) for products purchased at Barnes & Noble College bookstores that are listed for sale in the Barnes & Noble Booksellers inventory management system.

Opened music CDs/DVDs/audio books may not be returned, and can be exchanged only for the same title and only if defective. NOOKs purchased from other retailers or sellers are returnable only to the retailer or seller from which they are purchased, pursuant to such retailer's or seller's return policy. Magazines, newspapers, eBooks, digital downloads, and used books are not returnable or exchangeable. Defective NOOKs may be exchanged at the store in accordance with the applicable warranty.

Returns or exchanges will not be permitted (i) after 14 days or without receipt or (ii) for product not carried by Barnes & Noble or Barnes & Noble.com.

Policy on receipt may appear in two sections.

Return Policy

With a sales receipt or Barnes & Noble.com packing slip, a full refund in the original form of payment will be issued from any Barnes & Noble Booksellers store for returns of undamaged NOOKs, new and unread books, and unopened and undamaged music CDs, DVDs, and audio books made within 14 days of purchase from a Barnes & Noble Booksellers store or Barnes & Noble.com with the below exceptions:

A store credit for the purchase price will be issued (i) for purchases made by check less than 7 days prior to the date of return, (ii) when a gift receipt is presented within 60 days of purchase, (iii) for textbooks, or (iv) for products purchased at Barnes & Noble College bookstores that are listed for sale in the Barnes & Noble Booksellers inventory management system.

Opened music CDs/DVDs/audio books may not be returned, and can be exchanged only for the same grows. Fish don't try to swim, they just swim. Flowers don't try to bloom, they bloom. Birds don't try to fly, they fly. This is their intrinsic nature. The earth doesn't try to spin on its own axis; it is the nature of the earth to spin with dizzying speed and to hurtle through space. It is the nature of babies to be in bliss. It is the nature of the sun to shine. It is the nature of the stars to glitter and sparkle. And it is human nature to make our dreams manifest into physical form, easily and effortlessly.[1]

Let's be honest—control only gets us so far. By insisting on managing every aspect of a situation, we eliminate any possibility that something unexpected or miraculous will occur. In fact, sometimes we're faced with problems that are literally impossible to resolve through control, and at these times we have no choice but to let go and allow. A few years ago, Christy found herself in such a situation, and to this day we are both still amazed at how flawlessly the universe provided a resolution:

> *Let's be honest—control only gets us so far. By insisting on managing every aspect of a situation, we eliminate any possibility that something unexpected or miraculous will occur.*

---

[1] Chopra, *The Seven Spiritual Laws of Success*, 53.

A *few years ago* I was doing a lot of speaking at colleges all over the United States, which required me to travel almost every week. On one of my trips from the States back home to Canada, I lost my Pennsylvania driver's license. I looked at my schedule for the following week and saw that I was scheduled to speak at a college that was a nine-hour drive from the Kansas City airport.

Knowing that I wouldn't be able to rent a car without a driver's license, I looked into public transportation options, but none of them would get me where I needed to be in time. The more I struggled to come up with a solution for the situation the more anxious I became; I just couldn't fathom a way to make it happen.

Finally, I left the airline tickets on my desk and went out for a short walk. When I came back I looked at the tickets more carefully and noticed for the first time that I had a one-hour layover—in Philadelphia! This piece of information provided a glimpse of the solution: go to the Philadelphia DMV and get a duplicate license. Of course, I had no idea how I was going to make it work. In fact, I realized that there really was no way that *I* could make it work. The only way to pull this off, I decided, would be to turn the entire situation over to the forces that be. Taking a few deep breaths, I literally envisioned handing this dilemma over to a power greater than myself.

As my husband drove me to the airport early that Wednesday morning, I said out loud, "Okay, universe, I have no idea how this is going to happen. I cannot and will not force it to happen, but I trust that everything will come together in perfect timing. You know my intention; I now place the execution of it in your hands." I felt my shoulders instantly relax and my mind quiet.

My plane touched down in Philadelphia at exactly 11:30 A.M. I calmly walked through the baggage claim area and hailed the one and only cab that happened to be waiting. En route from the airport to the DMV, the driver commented on the lack of usual weekday traffic. "Interesting," I said, and continued to actively surrender any desire to try to control the situation.

Now, if you've ever had the pleasure of visiting a DMV during lunch hour, you know that it's almost always packed with people. But amazingly enough, there was not a single person ahead of me in line. I approached the window to apply for a duplicate license and encountered a hitch: I needed a money order to complete the transaction. Unflustered, I walked across the street, bought the money order, and ten minutes later was back in the cab with my temporary license in hand.

We pulled up to the Philadelphia airport at exactly 12:20 P.M.—the entire event had taken less than fifty minutes. I walked through security, again surprised and delighted to find no one in line, and arrived at my gate in time to call Rebecca, the one person who I knew would completely understand what just unfolded.

* * *

We love this story because it so beautifully illustrates the Law of Allowing in action. By setting a clear intention of the outcome we desire and then allowing things to unfold naturally and spontaneously, it's as though the floodgates open wide and our goals are fulfilled in ways that our controlling minds never could have imagined. Ironically, allowing is actually one of the most powerful ways to make things happen.

Allowing Is Not Apathy

Over the years we have noticed that some high-achieving women have a tendency to confuse the Law of Allowing with an admission of subservience, passivity, or powerlessness. "Hey," our sharp, feisty clients are quick to retort, "we didn't get where we are in life by waiting for opportunities to fall in our laps!"

We're not suggesting that anyone's desires will be magically fulfilled by sitting around all day, "wishing" our way to success. It's more of a creative dance between us and the universe, and each must play its part. Our job is to set a clear intention of what we want; align our thoughts, beliefs, and energies with that intention; and remain open to receive it. It's the job of the universe to receive our signal and to deliver the life experiences that we've asked for, in perfect time.

There is no doubt that taking action is an important component in achieving any goal. But the trick is to know *when* to take action. When we try to take over the part that is meant for the universe, which many Alphas do, we not only slow down the creative process but we also wear ourselves out. Placing ourselves in an Allowing mindset actually accelerates the arrival of our desires—it opens us and makes us receptive, which is an essential ingredient in attracting what we want.

Allowing is anything but passive and it certainly should not be confused with weakness. *Weakness* is being so scared of the unknown that we try to fight a battle that is not ours to win; *strength* is keeping our attention focused on those things we can change, while allowing wiser and more capable forces to do the rest.

So how do we apply the Law of Allowing while remaining actively engaged in shaping our own destiny? We do it by investing our energy toward what we want to achieve, and yes, by taking concrete, measurable actions toward achieving it. But the critical difference between controlling and allowing reveals itself after we've done all we can do. The Controlling Alpha insists on managing when, where, and how the results she desires will come to pass, while the Allowing and Femininely Empowered Woman approach—the one Christy took that magical day in Philadelphia—is to step back and let the universe coordinate the details.

> **Weakness** *is being so scared of the unknown that we try to fight a battle that is not ours to win;* **strength** *is keeping our attention focused on those things we can change, while allowing wiser and more capable forces to do the rest.*

Allowing is a deliberate act of courage and faith—faith in ourselves, in others, and in life itself. It's affirming that we are safe even when we're not in control of every detail. This builds a well of resilience within us.

We develop maturity by learning to appreciate the built-in differences in every human being, and understanding that it's not our job to persuade others to conform to our preferences nor is it our business to manage what other people do or don't do. We learn to grant others—our children, spouses, loved ones, and even complete strangers—the freedom to be as they are and live how they choose.

Allowing doesn't mean that we have to agree with or approve of someone else's life choices. It means we recognize that every person has the right to determine his or her own destiny. Several years ago Christy's sister tragically took her own life, and while Christy will never approve of nor agree with her sister's choice, she has learned to accept it. This has given her the freedom to allow this event to be as it is without resisting or fighting against it.

Now you might be saying, "Sure, this sounds good in theory, but how can I allow in those moments when every fiber of my being is yearning for control?" It's true that learning to allow, rather than control, when things are not going your way takes some initial getting used to, so here are some guidelines to help you develop this muscle:

1. When you feel yourself starting to tense up about something that you perceive is not

going according to plan, relax, take a few deep breaths, and acknowledge that you are not alone, and that whether you feel it or not, there is an infinitely loving and benevolent universe working on your behalf.

2. As you breathe this in, see if you can find the willingness to let go and allow yourself to be led. The more you make this a daily practice, the easier it becomes to feel that Presence around and within you, and the more natural it will be to trust in and surrender to it. In fact, as you cultivate the allowing mindset, you'll get to the point where you no longer feel the need or desire to control others.

The chart that follows illustrates how a mindset of allowing can take you much farther and faster toward ultimate fulfillment than controlling ever could, and with much less effort and far greater joy. This is just a glimpse of what life looks like when viewed through the lens of allowing rather than controlling.

	When Operating from a Mindset of Controlling	When Embracing the Law of Allowing
How We Perceive Life	• Unsupportive • Scary • Difficult • Imperfect • Unmanageable and overwhelming	• Divinely guided • Safe • Easy and effortless • In perfect order • Supportive • Cocreative
How We Perceive Others	• Incompetent, incapable, and untrustworthy • Needing constant management and supervision	• Competent, capable, and trustworthy • Supportive and contributive • Sources of new ideas and approaches
How Others Perceive Us	• Critical • Dismissive and demanding • Closed • Rigid • Frantic • Arrogant	• Appreciative • Interested • Open to receive • Fluid and easygoing • Relaxed • Graceful
How We Feel	• Overwhelmed • Resentful • Burdened • Anxious and stressed • Isolated and alone • Angry	• Relaxed • Excited and invigorated • Free • Trusting • Connected and supported • Grateful, assured, and confident

By now it should be clear that allowing is an infinitely more powerful force than controlling ... so how exactly do we align ourselves with this powerful law? As you might have guessed, *trust* is the key that unlocks our resistance and shifts our energy from controlling to allowing.

Trust: The Key that Activates the Law of Allowing

Trust is a powerful force that disarms many of our anxieties; when we're drowning it's a life preserver that always brings us back to our inner core of stability. It's pretty simple, actually. The more trusting we are of our own inner resources, the less we feel we have to control and the more we activate the Law of Allowing. Learning to trust makes us more accepting of and receptive to whatever happens to arise, and infinitely more relaxed in the face of change.

Masculine energies such as assertiveness, control, and tenacity may set things into motion, but it's the feminine energies such as trust, surrender, and faith that enable us to receive and enjoy what we've generated. Trust creates the receptivity that allows the abundance we seek to flow through us easily and naturally. Sanaya Roman and Duane Packer state this simply and beautifully in their book entitled *Creating Money*:

> Trust is opening your heart, believing in yourself and in the abundance of the universe. It is knowing that the universe is

loving, friendly, and supports your higher good. Trust is knowing that you are part of the process of creating, and believing in your ability to draw to you what you want.[2]

In this universe, which is bound by time and space, there is always a delay between the conception of an idea and its manifestation. Trust is like an invisible link between the nonphysical world and the physical world. The moment we create an intention, its energy form already exists, but it's waiting for the perfect time to take physical form. Trust accelerates this process by softening our resistance and cultivating within us an easy, fluid vibration that brings our desires to life. The more we trust in the universe to handle the details, the more easily and naturally our desires flourish.

A seasoned gardener doesn't tug on a brand-new shoot to ensure its roots are thriving; she trusts the process that was set into motion the moment she planted the seed and waits patiently, knowing that, in time, her creation will bloom.

A seasoned gardener doesn't tug on a brand-new shoot to ensure its roots are thriving; she trusts the process that was set into motion the moment she planted the seed and waits patiently, knowing that, in time, her creation will bloom. In the same way, we can alleviate our fears and overcome our addiction to control

[2] Sanaya Roman and Duane Packer, *Creating Money* (Tiburon, CA: H. J. Kramer, 1988), 109.

by remembering that we are supported by the same unseen force. We trust that we will be taken care of, even if we don't always know how or by whom.

Through deep, abiding faith in this benevolent force, we begin to know that no matter what happens in our lives, all is unfolding for the betterment of ourselves. Mind you, this level of faith isn't always easy to uphold when life gets rocky—when we experience financial hardship, we lose a loved one, or our child is hurt. At times like these, it's easy to question the "forces that be" and conclude that life is safer under our own direction: *What were you thinking, God? Anybody up there watching out for me?* Like a three-year-old who may not understand why her parents take away some of her Halloween candy, we may not always understand why negative things happen to us. The parents know that what may disappoint their child today will ultimately keep her healthy (and her dentist happy) tomorrow. Developing the faith that "everything in life is happening *for* me and not *to* me" eases the pain when the unexpected or the unimaginable occurs.

Shifting our thoughts from fear to trust, we begin to look for the opportunities in the midst of challenges. We wonder how we will grow because of the struggles we are experiencing. As Emmanuel Teney, a professor of psychiatry at Wayne State University, says, "As your faith is strengthened you will find that there is no longer the need to have a sense of control, that things will flow as they will, and that you will flow with them, to your great delight and benefit." By practicing resting in unwavering faith, the quality of our lives vastly increases, and we enjoy ourselves more thoroughly because we're relaxed and present. And we allow more abundance to flow to us and through us.

Cultivating Trust

It's important to realize that trust is not an "all or nothing" proposition. There are many areas of life where we are very trusting, and in these areas control is seldom an issue. But there are other areas where our knuckles are practically white from gripping so tightly. For example, we may trust ourselves to be conscientious and involved parents, but have no faith whatsoever in our ability to look after our own health and well-being. We might have complete faith in our husband's fidelity and yet forbid him to go anywhere near the checkbook. To unleash the power of the Law of Allowing in all aspects of our lives, we have to sniff out the places where we're still in resistance. Are we still driven by the belief that if we don't take matters into our own hands and anticipate every possible outcome, bad things will happen? Of course, common sense still applies. The Law of Allowing doesn't give us license to override our better judgment. If your husband is a gambler, or has proven to be irresponsible with money, you'll naturally think twice before handing over the ATM card! Trusting our inner wisdom to know when and whom to trust is the best way to stay out of resistance and in alignment with the Law of Allowing.

Developing trust where you feel the most vulnerable takes time and deliberative action, but you can do it. It's actually easier than trying to control everything—it's like walking without weights strapped to your legs. Think about it. We've had plenty of practice flexing our control muscles; now it's time to lighten our load by learning the art of letting go. When we move from controlling to allowing, life gets easier, and so much more fun. We finally have the freedom to leave our to-do lists behind and let the cards fall where they may.

We can let our partners take the lead every now and then and enjoy the new directions they may take us. We can trust the people around us to get their jobs done well without constantly having to look over their shoulders. Most importantly, as we begin to rest in the certainty that everything is happening for our greater good, life becomes carefree and joy-filled. Relationships are more harmonious, and we produce results with more ease. All manner of magic unfolds when we allow ourselves to live in the mystery. The formula is this: As you trust more, you control less. The less you control, the less you resist. The less you resist, the more easily you receive everything for which you've been asking.

When we move from controlling to allowing, life gets easier, and so much more fun. We finally have the freedom to leave our to-do lists behind and let the cards fall where they may.

The following exercise will help to identify beliefs that keep you from allowing life to unfold gracefully.

Bitch Tips for Trusting

- Remind yourself that life always has a way of working out for the best. Think of an example, in the recent or distant past, where what first seemed like a problem or a curse turned out to be a blessing.
- Make a list of all the times when life *has* supported you—a friend called just when you felt like breaking down, your husband picked up dinner on the night you were working late, your business partner faxed you the document you left at work, your neighbor rolled out your trash cans when you forgot to do it before leaving town.

EXERCISE
Transforming Controlling into Allowing

Set aside twenty to thirty minutes of uninterrupted time to complete this exercise, making sure that you have a journal or a piece of paper and pen nearby to record any insights or actions that may arise.

    To begin, allow yourself to recall a recent experience when you actually caught yourself in the act of trying to control something or someone. It might have been when you were at work, out with friends, or at home with your husband and kids. Replay it as if it were happening now. As vividly as you can, picture the people involved in the situation and the circumstances that led up to it. What strategies did you use to take control? Were your tactics overt or passive-aggressive? Be as honest with yourself as you can and write down whatever details you can recall.

Remembering that all attempts at control are driven by fear, see if you can recall what you were feeling in that moment. Give yourself permission to be vulnerable and feel the underlying insecurity that triggered your controlling behavior. Ask yourself, "What was I afraid of?" and allow yourself to hear whatever answers arise. Allow yourself to feel the ineffectiveness of control. How frustrating is it when your attempts to influence a situation don't work, or worse, when they backfire? Feel the powerlessness that comes from trying to manage someone other than yourself.

Listen for the thoughts that triggered these emotions. Be gentle and patient with yourself as you write them down.

Now, let yourself go deeper into the core belief that generates these thoughts. Slowly allow this underlying belief to reveal itself. How do you feel as you hold this belief? Do you feel scared and vulnerable? Anxious or unprotected?

As you consider this underlying belief, ask yourself what new belief you could hold that would make you feel more relaxed and at ease. What statements could you affirm that would lead to more empowering behaviors? Try these out and see how they feel:

* *I know that I am supported in wonderful and un-expected ways.*
* *I am open to receive the blessings that abound.*
* *I trust in a loving and bountiful universe to fulfill my every need.*
* *I allow abundance to flow through me.*
* *I integrate trust into every aspect of my life.*

Write down your new belief statement in your journal and allow it to become deeply anchored in your consciousness by saying it a few times out loud. Allow yourself to fully embody the meaning of this statement.

Now ask yourself what actions you could take—right now or in the future—to align your behaviors with this new belief statement. Could you:

* *Delegate more?*
* *Cross something off your list in favor of taking some much-needed downtime?*

Write down whatever ideas come to you, making sure that the actions you choose are not dependent upon the approval or participation of anyone else.

Allow yourself to feel the way you would feel if you actually took those actions. Would you be more relaxed? More at ease? Make a commitment to take this action and to remind yourself of your new empowering belief statement several times throughout your day, each time feeling the truth of this statement.

With your next breath, consciously and deliberately release the rest. Give yourself permission to let go of what you can't control. Take a few moments to savor this feeling.

• • • • • • • • • • • • • •

Go to www.alphabitchbook.com to download an additional "Allowing" meditation, and use the authorization code TYABFREE.

Bitch Tip

Feeling the stress of micromanaging everyone else's behaviors? Take a deep breath and let go, knowing there's a force much greater than you (and them) guiding your way. Your only job is to surrender and allow.

chapter three
The Competitive Alpha

If there's one thing that makes a true Alpha Bitch bare her teeth, it's competition. In fact, nothing gets this woman's juices flowing more than hearing about the accomplishments or acquisitions of another female. We sometimes joke that the Competitive Alpha has 20/20 peripheral vision because she is constantly looking over her shoulder to see who is doing what and who might be poised to outdo her in some way.

When an Alpha Bitch perceives herself as being in the lead, she feels smug and energized. But when she finds herself coming up short next to her competitors, she is likely to become withdrawn or depressed or lash out in a jealous rage. Life for this woman is a perpetual game, and she is obsessed with keeping score. She has to prove that she is the best at everything, from the shape of her body to the size of her diamond ring to the prestige of the position she holds at work. Only after she's made it clear that she's the one with the more successful husband, the bigger home, or the most perfect Downward Facing Dog pose does she feel content.

Monica Geller, the slightly neurotic and highly competitive character on the sitcom *Friends* portrays the Competitive Alpha. Her cast of twentysomething pals puts up with her crazy competitive nature, even when she's completely out of control. If you're a fan of the show like we are, you might remember the Thanksgiving-day football game where she remained on the field long after the food was gone and everyone else left because she would not let her brother claim the football that determined the winning touchdown (and, of course, the coveted "Geller Cup"). Or there was the "Scrabble incident" where she actually threw the board at one of her friends because she was losing the game. Our favorite episode is when she finds out that she gives terrible massages. The idea that she's not the best at everything she does drives her completely crazy. In order to appease her, Chandler says, "You give the best *worst* massages. If there were a trophy for worst massages, you would get it!" This does the trick, and her insanely competitive drive is quieted … at least for the moment.

At work, the Competitive Alpha's fierce nature is expected. After all, business is one area that celebrates a competitive drive. In small doses, she could be considered an asset; her hyper-ambitious nature may spark others to excel and her need to beat out the competition may benefit those who employ her. But when that tenacity turns into obsession, her fierce competitive drive may steer her straight off the cliff. For instance, the Competitive Alpha who is afraid of losing her hard-earned job status will go out of her way to prevent others from advancing. She becomes the gatekeeper, ferociously defending her turf against any perceived interloper.

Or, in her quest to dominate the industry, she soaks up all the information offered to her by a fair-minded mentor, whom she then betrays. She will seize any opportunity to move her superior out and move herself in. The Competitive Alpha at work is neither afraid of doing whatever it takes to advance nor apologetic. She can be ruthless—shoving past coworkers, alienating clients, and proving to be more disruptive than beneficial.

Even in her intimate relationships, the Competitive Alpha feels the need to outshine her partner. Just watch how quickly she steals the spotlight away from her man if friends seem more interested in him. She'll talk over him, finish telling his stories, and make sure that she gets the loudest laughs and the most attention. Should he get a promotion at work, or a salary increase, her competitive wheels start spinning trying to figure out how she can advance, too. Rather than encouraging her partner or celebrating his victories, his successes quickly become fuel for her "outdo-him-at-all-costs" attitude. Any extracurricular activities they share together become a challenge to see who can win—who runs the farthest, snow skis the fastest, or serves up the snazziest tennis swing. She may even compete for their kids' affection. If they seek comfort in their daddy, she views this as a threat—or worse—as a direct affront. "I carried that child for nine months," she fumes. "Why would she want you?"

The Competitive Alpha may even resort to comparing her partner to men she thinks are better than him. "Why can't he make more money like my friend's husband?" Or, "Why can't he be as affectionate as my sister's boyfriend?" Or, "Cindy's husband, Tom, is so smart, I should be with someone like him." Her competitive urge can spill over and drown him, leaving him feeling inadequate, incapable, and resentful.

As a mother, the Competitive Alpha will make certain that her children are front and center. They must have the lead roles in school plays, top honors for each grade, and star positions in each sport. She'll go out of her way to tell you how her kids were the first to potty train, sleep through the night, learn their ABCs, or get accepted into prestigious schools. She constantly brags about her kids' accomplishments to anyone who will listen—and to those who would rather not! It's infuriating to watch how far she'll go to keep up with your kids. Mention that your daughter just started ballet lessons with a noted instructor and her little Chelsea will be enrolled in the class before sundown. If your son made varsity basketball, her Andrew will be out until midnight shooting free throws.

It's not only through her children that her competitive streak is exposed. *She* must be the best—the most organized, the thinnest, the best dressed, and the most liked by the other moms. Her house has to be the cleanest, her husband the most supportive, and her lifestyle the most envied. This puts tremendous pressure on her family to be perfect, and it definitely weighs heavily on her shoulders. She's the mom who shows up at the playgroup perfectly put together, complete with an overly cheery attitude and a truckload of homemade, sugar-free snacks for the entire group. Meanwhile, you can't be sure if you brushed your teeth or changed out of the shirt with baby spit on it. And, oh by the way, your kids will be snacking on store-bought gummy worms—the sugar-filled, nutrient-free variety. Next to her, your bad attire, bad attitude, and bad breath scream *bad mom*!

Among her friends, the Competitive Alpha's behaviors are notorious, the stuff of which reality television is made. To make sure that she would look better in your jeans than you do, she hits the gym hard every morning, keeping her tight physique. She'll campaign vigorously to be the friend everybody turns to for advice. She may even risk going into debt if it means her jewelry, clothes, and handbags draw the most attention when she is out with a group of friends.

The Competitive Alpha is so skilled in the art of one-upmanship that she may not even realize she's doing it. Tell her how excited you are about your upcoming Mediterranean cruise and she'll remind you that she was there, too, on a bigger ship, of course. Give her the inside scoop about a sale you just found and she'll have one of everything you bought before nightfall. Share with her your dreams and aspirations and she'll find a way to beat you to them. It's not her intention to hurt you; in fact, she's probably not even aware that she's stealing your thunder. Being number one is so ingrained in her that all she registers is the intense need to one-up everyone. The drive to be the best at everything overrides common sense and social graces.

Let the Games Begin...

Because her happiness is intimately tied to being number one, the Competitive Alpha works extremely hard to win that title. And she can be downright cutthroat when defending her position. Although most Alphas have enough self-restraint to stop before things get "down and dirty," there is always that one woman whose competitive hunger is so insatiable that she will resort to underhanded measures. For example, she might "accidentally" forget to relay an important message to a coworker or snub a good friend in favor of securing a place for herself in a more desirable social circle. She may target the colleague whose career is advancing faster than her own, seeking ways to outdo her on a personal level in an attempt to feel better about herself. If she's desperate enough, she may even stop by your home wearing her shortest miniskirt to ask your husband if he'll help her hang the Christmas lights.

Just tune into any episode of *The Real Housewives* and you'll see how the Competitive Alpha's perfectly manicured claws come out. Some of these women are brutal in their tactics. And although most women may not resort to these levels of competition, we all have to admit we've "gone there" a time or two. To see where you fall on the Competitive Alpha Bitch scale, take the quiz below:

THE COMPETITOR—ARE YOU THIS TYPE OF ALPHA BITCH?

1. *When you lose a game of tennis to a female friend, you . . .*

    A   Feel proud that you played hard and got a good workout.
    B   Make excuses for your performance—a bad night's sleep, an antiquated racquet, or an old college injury acting up.

C   Congratulate her, but point out that you beat her the last two times you played.

D   Look for a new tennis partner.

2. *When your longtime neighbors announce that they're selling their house and moving to a more affluent community, you ...*

A   Wish them well and make a play for their old patio furniture.

B   Feel relief that you're not taking on a mortgage that size.

C   Suddenly find your quaint home small and dreary, and begin dreaming about a major remodel.

D   Decide your family should move to an even more affluent neighborhood than them, even if it means living beyond your means.

3. *When a good friend boasts that her three-year-old son (or grandson) is already playing concertos on the piano, you ...*

A   Congratulate her for passing on her outstanding genetics and let it go.

B   Quickly recite your little one's Top Ten life accomplishments, even if paste eating tops the list.

C   Log on to the computer the moment you get home to locate a crash course in cello or Mandarin Chinese.

D   Remind yourself that children express their brilliance at different stages and in different ways.

4. *You're headed out to lunch with a coworker who insists on driving so she can show off her brand-new BMW. As she's gushing about all its features, you ...*

A   Roll down the window, crank up the sound system, and yell, "Road trip!"

B   Compliment her on her new purchase while making an underhanded remark about the damage she's doing to the ozone layer, or remind her that a Mercedes is a much better car.

C   Console yourself by thinking about all the debt she's accruing.

continued on next page ...

continued . . .

D   Bring up a topic that you know makes her uncomfortable to knock her off her high horse.

5. *You're going to a party with a friend and when she arrives at your house to pick you up, she's wearing a super-sexy dress. You . . .*

A   Get inspired and ask her to help you kick your outfit up a notch.

B   Tell her she looks great, then gossip about her when you get to the party.

C   Give her your longest trench coat to put on, with a word of caution that it's wicked cold outside.

D   Change into something you're really not comfortable in, just so you won't be outdone.

6. *When the umpire at your son's Little League game makes a questionable call that denies him of what could have been a perfect defensive inning, you . . .*

A   Are initially upset, but decide to use it as an opportunity to explain that bad calls are part of life.

B   Offer a single snide remark in the direction of the umpire, then let it go.

C   Dwell on the incident to the point of a) missing the rest of the game; b) annoying the other parents; c) embarrassing your son; ⁻or d) all of the above!

D   Storm the field and strip the ump of his duties (and his masculinity)!

7. *When you see your college roommate for the first time in more than a year, you're stunned that she's no longer a size 12, but a size 6. After the initial shock wears off, you . . .*

A   Seize the first opportunity to ask her about her healthful eating and exercise strategies.

B   Refuse all food and obsess about her all evening, even though you're supposed to be celebrating your reunion with old friends.

C   Offer to do all the cooking and add copious amounts of butter to your friend's food.

D   Bring your intellectual A-game to every conversation. You may not be the thinnest, but you're determined to prove that you're the smartest.

8.   *You and a girlfriend started working for a company at the same time, but because she hired a nanny to care for her child while you took a year off to care for yours, she has since been promoted to an executive position. You ...*

A   Feel fortunate to have a long history and good rapport with one of your superiors.

B   Have a hard time respecting her new position of authority, but work well with her nonetheless.

C   Begrudge her for fast-tracking her career but keep quiet in order to save face.

D   Question her values in front of other coworkers by telling them she chose work over family.

9.   *Over dinner one evening, one of your good friends gets a little too friendly with your husband, so you ...*

A   Let it go for the time being, but tell her later on that her behavior made you uncomfortable.

B   Say nothing, but give her a really dirty look.

C   Start flirting with her husband to see how she likes it.

D   Tell everyone except your friend about the incident, and caution them to "hang on to their husbands" whenever she's around.

10.   *While on a casual hike with a group of friends, you notice one woman is consistently at the head of the pack. You ...*

A   Let her take the lead; she'll warn everyone about the loose gravel and slippery spots!

continued on next page ...

continued ...

B Interpret her walking ahead to mean that she thinks she's in better shape and resolve to show her she's not.

C Use the time at the rear of the pack to catch up with friends.

D Secretly wish that she would fall and land in poison oak.

SCORING KEY:

1. a-1, b-3, c-4, d-5 • 2. a-1, b-2, c-4, d-5 • 3. a-1, b-4, c-5, d-2 • 4. a-1, b-4, c-3, d-5 • 5. a-1, b-4, c-3, d-5 6. a-1, b-3, c-4, d-5 • 7. a-1, b-3, c-5, d-4 • 8. a-1, b-2, c-4, d-5 • 9. a-1, b-3, c-4, d-5 10. a-2, b-3, c-1, d-5

ASSESSMENT:

Using the number that corresponds to each answer you gave, add up the total number of points.

If you scored 20 or fewer points, rest assured that although you might have some Competitive Alpha characteristics, you don't manifest them through competition.

If you scored between 21 and 35 points, odds are high that your fixation on what other women do or have is diluting your own creativity.

If you scored between 35 and 50 points, you're most likely exhausted from constantly comparing yourself with—and pitting yourself against—other women. In this chapter, you'll learn how to use the synergistic effect of collaboration to more effortlessly attract success into your life, while allowing others to do the same.

We All Do It, but Why?

Competition among females is a dirty little secret that few of us are willing to admit. Women don't want to talk about it for fear that we'll reinforce the stereotype that we're mean and catty, and men don't want to talk about it because they don't want to come across as being sexist. Yet many of us act this way, know someone who does, and/or have had someone interact with us in this unpleasant manner.

From a distance, we may dislike or even envy this woman, who appears to have it all and is definitely not shy about flaunting it, but to understand *why* she behaves the way she does requires us to look a bit deeper.

The competitive mindset is based on a flawed belief that to be good enough we have to prove that we're

> *Insecurity and insufficiency are the hidden mechanisms that drive us to compete rather than collaborate. Winning may give us a temporary sense of value and significance, but in the absence of genuine self-love, we are continually driven to search outside ourselves for evidence of our intrinsic value, and as a result, even if we succeed, we're never satisfied.*

the best—and that allowing others to shine will somehow diminish our own light. Because we feel so deeply threatened, we view other women as opponents, enemies, and rivals, rather than partners and confidantes. Insecurity and insufficiency are the hidden mechanisms that drive us to compete rather than collaborate. Winning may give us a temporary sense of value and significance, but in the absence of genuine self-love, we are continually driven to search outside ourselves for evidence of our intrinsic value, and as a result, even if we succeed, we're never satisfied.

Winning the Battle but Losing the War

The admiration we gain through competitive tactics may infuse us with a temporary sense of worth, but the feeling never lasts. In order to sustain this false self-esteem, we must continually find and "beat" new opponents. And to make matters worse, our hunger for recognition and approval is often so intense that it blinds us to the effects of our own behavior. It's not until we've lost the respect of our workmates or the loyalty of our friends that we grasp the true price we pay for being so competitive.

The Competitive Alpha in the Workplace

In the workplace, our competitive drive can be so strong that we find ourselves resorting to underhanded or destructive measures in order to advance our careers. Although we may justify our actions by telling ourselves it's "just business," our cutthroat tactics ultimately compromise our integrity. In most industries, reputation is everything. When we are more invested in beating out our opponents than we are in contributing to the overall success of our careers, we not only jeopardize our reputation but the company's reputation as well. Wary about our ethics, clients may ask to work with another colleague, or seek out another organization all together. Coworkers fed up with our antics may go out of their way to be assigned to projects that don't involve us. Our Competitive Alpha approach may win us a sale or two, or a bigger promotion, but if it discredits our name in the process, where's the long-term gain? *No Where*

Bitch Tips for Competitive Colleagues

- Focus on doing your job to the best of your ability and resist the urge to see what others are accomplishing.
- Remember that the Competitive Alpha's need for acknowledgment arises from insecurity not confidence. By affirming your talents and accomplishments, you quell the insecurities
- Reach out to your colleagues and connect. Sharing ideas and benefiting from one another's strengths helps keep the creative sparks flying.

The Competitive Alpha as a Partner

Competition drives a mighty wedge in the intimacy we share with our partners. Rather than acting as teammates, we often treat one another like adversaries. As innocent as the bickering may seem, over time those little jabs can squeeze the goodwill out of our relationships. Power struggles and backbiting pit us against each other and make rivals out of lovers. We wonder why he withholds his feelings from us, or acts so guarded when we're around. It's because competition pushes him away while limiting both his willingness and his ability to open up and tell us what he's thinking. After all, if we're quick to snatch his successes away from him by constantly one-upping him, gloat at his expense when he falls short of our expectations, or downplay his achievements by rolling our eyes and acting indifferent, why would he want to share either his triumphs or his deepest concerns? In fact, we're probably the last person with whom he feels safe enough to be vulnerable. Sure, we may feel a temporary sense of superiority, but at what cost? Remember, you're on the same team so when you bring him down a few notches (self-satisfying as that may be), you lower yourself—and your partnership—as well.

Bitch Tips for Competitive Partners

- Make it a habit to build your partner up, not tear him down. Find every reason to appreciate him, not just for what he does but for who he is.
- When you overhear others complimenting your partner, join in and agree. This is a perfect opportunity to admire the person you chose.
- Share the love. If others are praising *you*, don't forget to include him. Next time your mom compliments you on a lovely dinner, let her know that he did all the shopping and chopping.

- Start thinking of each other as teammates. Make a list of all the ways you enhance each other's lives and are stronger because of the union.
- Stop comparing him to other men. Love him for who he *is*, rather than critiquing him for who he's *not*.

The Competitive Alpha as a Mother

As mothers, asking our children to be the best at everything they do is unfair and places too much pressure on them to be perfect. It robs them of their childhoods and the freedom to enjoy their activities without constant worry. Expecting the best may seem like an acceptable method to head our children toward excellence. But there's a difference between seeing and celebrating the best in our children and feverishly demanding perfection from them. When our competitive needs spill over onto our children, we change the people they are. They start becoming as anxious and driven as us, thinking they are only as good as their latest accomplishments. They may grow up feeling they have to be perfect to prove themselves worthy of our love. Of course, they will eventually tire of our constant need for more, and resent the pressure we put on them. But the saddest consequence of our unrelenting need to see them "win at all costs" is that our children will feel as if they're never good enough. Their focus will always rest on their few failings, not their many accomplishments.

Bitch Tips for Competitive Alpha Moms

- Stop and question your motives when pushing your kids. Ask yourself, "Is this really for them or for me?"
- Let your child's actions stand on her own without comparison. When she brings home her grades, don't ask how the other kids did or mention that her older brother got an A in that class.
- If you catch yourself competing with another parent, stop yourself and offer her praise instead. Compliment the way she braids her daughter's hair or handles her son's tantrums.
- Take a moment to reflect on the qualities that make you a good parent and really soak them in.
- Remember that the two best gifts we can give our kids are unconditional love and acceptance. Lavish them with plenty of both.

The Competitive Alpha as a Friend

Competition in friendships can have deeply corrosive effects. Our closest girlfriends should be those we can turn to for support and guidance. We count on their honest feedback: Is this skirt too short? Should I color my hair? Do I have something in my teeth? But when jealousy and competition enter this bond, the person's opinion we have grown to rely upon becomes too distorted to be trusted. We hear so many women say that they're more comfortable in the company of men than other women. They tell us how tired they are of the catty, competitive barbs they receive from their gal pals—and who can blame them? Sure, measuring ourselves against our girlfriends is natural and may prompt us to excel. But when our Competitive Alpha compels us to be better than her in all ways, it sours the bonds we share.

Competition and jealousy can bring out fierce aggressive emotions within us. We may lash out in anger or spite when our Top Dog title is threatened, humiliating ourselves and those around us, all to ensure we are the best. But what happens when we feel we can't win—we won't ever be as smart, as witty, as thin, or as successful as our girlfriend? If we're a Competitive Alpha, this signals defeat. Collapsing in on ourselves, we become mired in self-loathing and self-doubt. These painful feelings are then wrongly interpreted as a warning: keep our friends at arm's length, separating us from the camaraderie of our girlfriends and leaving us feeling isolated and alone. Even if we count many women among our friends, the quality of closeness we share with them is compromised by the suspicion and resentment that competitiveness breeds. We simply can't receive the many gifts that female friendships offer when we're constantly viewing them as our rivals. Jealousy robs us of the ability to support other

Jealousy robs us of the ability to support other women in realizing their dreams, and to allow them to support us in the realization of our own.

women in realizing their dreams, and to allow them to support us in the realization of our own.

Bitch Tips for Competitive Alpha Friends

- Celebrate your friends' victories. If a close girlfriend
  just lost twenty pounds, bought a great house, earned
  a nice promotion, or found the love of her life, go wild
  for her. Let her success inspire you. As you do, your
  own dreams will be fulfilled that much faster.
- Ask for her help rather than excluding her because
  she lost her baby weight and is now making you feel
  pudgy, or because she's engaged and you're still looking. Provided she's not a Competitive Alpha (and if
  she is, feel free to leave a copy of this book on her
  doorstep), she'll be thrilled to support you in accomplishing your goals.
- Regularly acknowledge your own talents and successes (we tend to focus only on the failures). Saving cards
  and letters of appreciation sent to you by friends, family members, and clients is a perfect way to remind
  yourself that you are loved and valued.
- Look around and validate yourself for all of the wonderful things you've created—the lovely home you
  live in, your beautiful children, your supportive and
  caring husband, your loving family. All these achievements, while they don't define you, provide a nice reminder of your creative capacity.

When our number-one goal is to be richer, smarter, thinner, or prettier than the people around us, our center of gravity shifts and our power is given to people, situations, and circumstances outside of ourselves.

To put it simply, it's much harder to hit our own targets when we're marking the progress of others. How can we possibly stay focused on the business at hand when we're overly concerned with what others are doing? Not only does our fixation with where we are in relation to someone else diminish our productivity but it's also incredibly exhausting. Let's face it—scheming, plotting, backstabbing, and sabotaging others to make sure that we stay at the head of the pack takes a lot out of us! It's like running a never-ending marathon. When we fall into the Competitive Alpha trap, we fail to realize that pitting ourselves against others only ends up diffusing our own creative power. Because we are so busy focusing our creative power on comparison and competition, we have very little time or energy left over to invest in enriching and enjoying our own lives.

> *Because we are so busy focusing our creative power on comparison and competition, we have very little time or energy left over to invest in enriching and enjoying our own lives.*

It is an indisputable universal law that what we focus on expands. This means that when we are consumed with what others have—and what we don't—we are giving attention to and enhancing all that we feel is inferior or missing from our lives.

✳ Remember the manifestation formula? Our thoughts, together with our emotions, create our energetic field. And it is from this field that we attract people and circumstances into our lives. Competing and comparing ourselves to others drops our energetic vibe from happy, enthusiastic, and excited to anxious, desperate, and even resentful—emotions that block the abundance we seek by clinging to (and keeping us in) a state of lack. When we are in Competitive Alpha mode, we go from open and allowing to closed and restricting faster than we can say, "They have a better *what*?"

Always chasing the next victory means we miss out on the very experiences that make life worth living. Consider the following:

- How many moments of true enjoyment with your children slipped by unnoticed because you were preoccupied with how well your parenting skills measured up against those of other mothers?

- How many opportunities have you missed at work because your mind was working overtime figuring out how to make yourself more recognized than another coworker?

- How many times have you refused support from another woman because you believed that accepting it would mean being perceived as weaker or inferior to her?

- How many possibilities for genuine friendship have you deprived yourself of because your ego was threatened by another woman's beauty, talent, or success?

Competition is based on the masculine paradigm that winning is prized above everything else. When we view the world through this lens, we operate from a "lone wolf" mindset that separates us from the resources, support, and camaraderie of the people around us. This not only adds to the load we carry on our shoulders but also leaves us feeling isolated and alone, rather than supported and connected. On the other hand, collaboration (the opposite force of competition) is based upon the feminine principles of interdependence, community, and connectedness—a state of being that we can all gain access to by understanding and applying the Law of Oneness.

> *Competition is based on the masculine paradigm that winning is prized above everything else ... Collaboration ... is based upon the feminine principles of interdependence, community, and connectedness.*

The Law of Oneness

The Law of Oneness recognizes the interconnectedness of all people and all things. It reminds us that we are all integral and inseparable parts of a vast universe. Ancient spiritual traditions have long held this to be true: every being is connected at the level of pure consciousness. Within every atom is life-force-energy, and this life-force-energy animates everything in the created universe, including ourselves. And although at the individual level we each have unique experiences and distinct outer expressions, at our essence, we are all one. In simple terms this means that there is what scientists call a "web of energy connecting all matter," and we are all part of this web.

In 1854, when Native American peacetime leader Chief Seattle surrendered his tribal lands to the governor of Washington, he made a speech noting that "humankind has not woven the web of life. We are but one thread within it. Whatever we do to the web, we do to ourselves. All things are bound together. All things connect." These words, like the Bible's commandment to "do unto others as we would have them do unto us," reflect a deep understanding of the interconnectedness of all things.

The Law of Oneness tells us that what we do to others, we do to ourselves, and that what affects one affects all. In other words, we cannot sit easy at the back of the boat unconcerned that the front of the boat is on fire, because literally and figuratively, we are all in the same boat!

We cannot compete with or wish harm to another person without adversely affecting ourselves in the process. Similarly, when we offer our support and generosity (whether in spirit or with more tangible resources), we are also positively affected by our giving. In a 1964 address, President John F. Kennedy stated, "As they say on my own Cape Cod, a rising tide lifts all the boats. And a partnership, by definition, serves both partners, without domination or unfair advantage."[1] The collaborative woman understands the Law of Oneness and uses it to her advantage. She knows that as females we are biologically wired to live in communion, not competition, with others. Regardless of whether we have ever given birth to a child, deep within every one of us is a powerful drive to care for and support the larger community of which we are a part. Men may be hunters who seek validation through their individual accomplishments, which the Alpha Bitch tries to emulate, but we empowered women feel our best and bring forth our best when we live and work together in tribes. Those of us who have been fortunate enough to experience female relationships that are untainted by competition can attest to this fact.

The Power of Connection

At our Goddess Retreats, we have the opportunity to witness the miracles that unfold when women come together to connect in love and support for one another—often for the very first time. For some, the experience of opening their hearts to other women facilitates a deep healing that gives them a firsthand experience of the power of choosing inclusion over division. Once they accept the shift from "me

---

[1] John F. Kennedy, address in the Assembly Hall at the Paulskirche, Frankfurt, West Germany, June 25, 1963, *Public Papers of the Presidents of the United States: John F. Kennedy* (Washington, DC: GPO, 1963), 519.

and mine" to "us and ours," their relationships with other women change radically.

This was exactly what happened for Rebecca, who many years ago had an experience of communing with other women that forever altered the dynamic of her close female friendships.

One summer when my son was three years old, my husband and I, along with four other families, decided to go on a camping trip together in Yosemite National Park in northern California. Now when I say camp, I mean *camp*. We were all roughing it, tent style, with few showers and virtually no amenities. To say that I was at first a bit skeptical of these arrangements would be an understatement. For three years I had been on nonstop, 24/7 Mommy Patrol and I knew how difficult it was to attend to every detail of child rearing, even with all the comforts of home to assist me. The thought of looking after my son in an unstructured and unpredictable environment was more than a little overwhelming as we wound our way up the mountain.

I have to tell you that in the twenty years that have passed since taking that trip, I have been on dozens of other vacations to far more luxurious destinations, but the week I spent in Yosemite still stands out in my heart and mind as one of the most enjoyable experiences I have ever had. Why? Because it was my first real taste of what I now understand as "tribal" living with a group of other women.

There were five women on the trip, all of us with young children, and within the first day of being there we seamlessly—almost wordlessly—fell into complete synchrony with one another. We shared the responsibilities around camp, which made all the usually mundane and tedious duties surprisingly pleasurable. We kept an eye on one another's kids so that each couple could slip away for a hike or enjoy some time together without a little one in tow. We took turns preparing meals and swapped recipes for dishes that I still savor to this day. It was the first time since my son had been born that I distinctly felt the weight of my motherhood responsibilities lifted from my shoulders. I knew that four other loving, competent women had my back, and it was heaven!

When the time came to pack up and go, you might have guessed that the women would be eager to get back to warm showers and comfy beds, but we were actually reluctant to leave. The camaraderie and support that we shared nourished us at such a deep level that none of us wanted it to end. We learned firsthand the benefits of building a strong community and the wisdom behind the old cliché that "it takes a village to raise a child." And while our husbands were certainly a vital part of the "village" we created in Yosemite that summer, it was the connection between the women that fed our hearts and souls.

I am forever grateful for that camping trip and for the women who experienced it along with me. I took everything I learned about collaboration back to my home and have continued to forge more intimate and meaningful connections with my female friends ever since.

* * *

Rebecca's experience perfectly illustrates that, as women, we are designed for camaraderie. We are at our best when we're working together, sharing responsibilities and resources, and benefiting from the different perspectives that come from confiding in one another our most cherished dreams, as well as our deepest concerns. But the moment our Competitive Alpha enters the picture, the trust that gives life to these connections is threatened. Fulfilling our highest potential as women and as individuals requires us to transform our behaviors from cutthroat and catty to collaborative and encouraging—and something remarkable happens when we do. We realize that all the energy that we had been using to hold each other back can be redirected to move us toward creating any outcome that we desire.

When we shift our focus from competition to collaboration, we can support the dreams and ideas of our friends, coworkers, partners, and kids as if they were our own. We're able to celebrate their victories fully and we can allow them to do the same for us. Most of all, we're able to receive the resources and support that others can provide, whether it's sharing in child care or work projects, or help-

> *As women, we are designed for camaraderie. We are at our best when we're working together, sharing responsibilities and resources, and benefiting from the different perspectives that come from confiding in one another our most cherished dreams, as well as our deepest concerns. But the moment our Competitive Alpha enters the picture, the trust that gives life to these connections is threatened.*

ing us to sort through personal issues that inevitably arise. We no longer have to go it alone or shoulder burdens in solitude; we can rely on our community to be there for us.

So, how can we support the dreams of our friends, family members, and colleagues when we share the same visions—we have our eye on the same single guy, or we're both up for the same promotion? Remember, in an unlimited universe the opportunities are endless. All possibilities exist when we align ourselves with the field of Pure Potentiality. So, it turns out that the guy your best friend is now dating (the guy you wanted to date) has several available, good-looking friends. And that promotion? It's one of many available in the company, not to mention all the other companies ready to advance empowered, abundant women like ourselves. The competitive mindset would have us believe that there is a limited supply of resources, and we'd better fight for our share. But the collaborative mindset is abundant. From this mindset we know that there is enough for everyone, and as one prospers, all prosper. Remember, a rising tide lifts all boats!

Collaboration is based on the understanding that asking for help is not a sign of weakness but a sign of wisdom. Reaching out to others acknowledges that we can accomplish more through working together than we could ever accomplish alone. Take a look at the chart that follows and see for yourself the benefits that come from embracing a mindset of collaboration.

	When Operating from Competition	When Embracing Collaboration
How We Perceive Life	• Limited in resources • "Dog eat dog" • Hostile	• Enough for all • Supportive • Easy and enjoyable
How We Perceive Others	• Rivals and opponents • Withholding and unwilling to share • Untrustworthy • Judgmental	• Ease our burdens • Supportive partners • Sharing and generous • Sources of inspiration
How Others Perceive Us	• Isolated and unapproachable • Guarded • Aggressive • Paranoid	• Helpful • Generous • Open and loving • Honest and transparent
How We Feel	• Alone • Insecure • Threatened • Burdened • Insignificant • Disconnected • Isolated	• Connected to self and others • Supported • Inspired • Enthusiastic • Open • Creative

Bitch Tips for Turning Competition into Collaboration

When you feel a jealous twinge, use it as an opportunity to fine-tune your own dreams. Just found out your girl-friend's heading to the Caribbean for two weeks? Let her plans spur you into booking that long overdue vacation you've always talked about with your husband, not to one-up her but to relax and reconnect with him. Your col-league just bagged a sweet promotion? Remind yourself that if he can do it, so can you. What is achieved by one opens up possibilities for all.

Inspiration: The Key That Activates the Law of Oneness

Now if you're like a lot of women you might believe that competing with your best friend to see who can drop ten pounds the fastest, or that placing a bet with a colleague at work over who closes the most sales, is a guaranteed way to create results. After all, competition does get your adrena-line flowing and the thought of winning can be a powerful incentive to take action, right? Yes—and no. What you have to understand is that competition is fear-based motivation that is more focused upon what you *don't* have than what you do. And because it's sourced from outside of you, it can't be internally sustained.

Competition is fear-based motivation that is more focused upon what you don't have than what you do. And because it's sourced from outside of you, it can't be internally sustained.

In other words, when you're measuring your progress against someone else's, your self-esteem is at the mercy of that person. In fact, your own feelings of worthiness are not even yours anymore—they're now variables that change according to the relative progress of someone else. If your best friend blows her diet, and you manage to stay true to yours, you feel good about yourself. But if she goes to the gym every day, while you're stuck at home with a sick child, you feel lousy.

The bottom line is that the intense fear-based rush of competition may fire you up in the short term but it will defeat you in the long run.

So what is the key that enables you to make the shift from competition to collaboration? The answer is simple: allow yourself to be inspired by, rather than jealous of, the accomplishments of other people.

Now just in case you're wondering, it's completely understandable to feel a twinge of jealousy when an old friend shows up sporting size 6 jeans when you're still wearing a nursing bra, or when a coworker earns the promotion that you were hoping to get. What's important to realize is that you do not have to allow this emotion to send you into a tailspin of competitive energy. If you can learn not to be jealous of another person's talents, but instead use them as inspiration to cultivate more of your own, you hold the key to transforming competition into collaboration, isolation into unity, and separation into oneness.

When you can view your relationship with others as a source of inspiration, you suddenly see their accomplishments as evidence that you are capable of creating that degree of fulfillment and more. When you can appreciate the affluence of another as proof that we live in an abundant universe, and that your share is just waiting for you to claim, you are now in the perfect mindset for achieving everything that you want.

When you come up against competitive feelings (which you will), you instantly recognize that they are arising because another person possesses something that you want for yourself. You wouldn't care that they had it if you didn't want it.

When you can appreciate the affluence of another as proof that we live in an abundant universe, and that your share is just waiting for you to claim, you are now in the perfect mindset for achieving everything that you want.

Rather than seething in bitterness or stagnating in victimization, you can use their accomplishments as a source of inspiration that helps you clarify what you want to create in your own life. The good news is that as rampant as competition is in our culture, especially female competition (and we should know—we wrote a book on it!), we are fortunate to have some powerful examples of successful women who demonstrate how to harness the power of collaboration.

Beloved television host, actress, and philanthropist Oprah Winfrey undoubtedly leads the pack of collaborative women. When Rosie O'Donnell won the Emmy Award for Most Outstanding Talk Show Host in the late 1990s, Oprah was the first to her feet to congratulate her. Years later, when a major network took a risk on comedian Ellen DeGeneres by making her the host of her own talk show, Oprah welcomed the new addition to daytime television and later surprised everyone by featuring Ellen on the cover of O, The Oprah Magazine.

In fact, "The Oprah Effect"—a term coined by Madison Avenue to describe her unprecedented ability to transform unknown start-up companies into brand names, and never-heard-of books into bestsellers—has farther-reaching effects than on just product sales alone. In the spirit of collaboration and noncompetitiveness, Oprah has launched the careers of dozens of stars including Dr. Phil, Rachael Ray, Dr. Oz, and Nate Berkus. Her generosity is a testament to the fact that sharing success with others attracts more of it to our lives than trying to hoard it for ourselves.

Collaboration generates a synergistic effect in which the sum is clearly greater than all its parts. In the same way that many hands make light work, helping others fulfill their dreams amplifies the energy we can invest toward our own; in the end, everybody wins when we pool our resources together. When we allow inspiration to transcend our competitive urges, life becomes easier, more enjoyable, and far less stressful.

Sure, our individual efforts are effective but they are multiplied a hundredfold when they are harmonized with those of others. Through collaboration we discover that working together takes us infinitely farther than working against one another.

The following journaling exercise will help to identify beliefs that keep you from embracing collaboration.

EXERCISE
Transforming Competition into Collabo   n

Set aside twenty to thirty minutes of uninte   d time to complete this exercise, making sure t   u have a journal or a piece of paper and pen nearby to record any insights or actions that may arise.

To begin, allow yourself to recall a recent experience when you actually caught yourself competing with someone. See if you can replay it as if it were happening in this moment. As vividly as you can, picture the people involved in the situation and the circumstances that led up to it. What were you saying or doing? What strategies were you using to appear better than someone else? Be as honest with yourself as you can, and write down whatever details you can recall.

Remembering that all competitive behaviors are driven by thoughts and feelings of fear and insufficiency, see if you can recall what you were feeling in that moment. Give yourself permission to be vulnerable and feel the underlying fears, doubts, and insecurities that triggered your competitive behavior.

Take a deep breath and try to go a little deeper. See if you can identify the thoughts that triggered your competitiveness. Take your time, give yourself permission to be completely honest, and write down as many thoughts as you can recall. Ask yourself, "What was I afraid of?" and allow yourself to hear whatever answer arises:

* *Were you afraid that if you didn't compete, you might lose something important to you?*
* *Were you operating from the belief that there simply isn't enough love, money, or other resources to go around?*
* *Did you feel insignificant if you weren't seen as the best?*

Now, remembering that all thoughts are generated from beliefs, allow yourself to trace those thoughts back to the core belief that ignited this competitive thinking. Be patient, simply allowing the belief to reveal itself in perfect time. Do you believe that you are not good enough?

How do you feel when you hold this limiting belief in your awareness? Does it make you feel unimportant, worthless, or insignificant? Describe what you experience as you replay this limiting belief and write it down in your journal.

As you consider the underlying belief that drove this behavior, ask yourself what new belief you could hold that would support you in feeling whole, complete, and perfect just as you are. What statements could you affirm to strengthen your self-esteem and soften your competitive urges? Try these on and see how they feel:

* *I am content with myself.*
* *My heart and mind are open to the endless opportunities available to me.*
* *I support myself and the people around me.*
* *I do not need to worry about what other people accomplish. I am on my own path.*
* *I trust in my creative abilities.*

As you identify a more empowering belief, write it down in your journal and allow it to become deeply anchored in your consciousness by saying it a few times out loud. Fully embody this statement.

Now consider what actions you could take—right now or in the future—to align your behaviors with this new belief. Could you reach out to another woman for guidance or support? Write down whatever ideas come to you.

Now allow yourself to feel the way you would feel if you actually took those actions. Would you be more open? More inspired? More lighthearted?

With your next breath, consciously and deliberately release any thoughts or feelings of competitiveness and allow yourself to feel how empowering it is as you state your new belief.

Make a commitment to remind yourself of your new empowering belief often, each time feeling the truth of the statement.

Take a moment to savor this feeling.

• • • • • • • • • • • • •

Go to www.alphabitchbook.com to download an additional meditation on releasing jealousy and competition, and use the authorization code TYABFREE.

Bitch Tip

Comparing yourself to someone else or consumed with jealous thoughts? Use that energy to your advantage by choosing inspiration over competition.

chapter four
The Disruptive Alpha

"As God is my witness, they're not going to lick me. I'm going to live through this and when it's all over, I'll never be hungry again… If I have to lie, cheat, steal, or kill, as God is my witness, I shall never be hungry again." These are the classic lines spoken by Scarlett O'Hara, the protagonist in the 1939 film *Gone with the Wind*. Words dripping with emotion, Scarlet's very presence screams "drama queen." Oh, the heightened emotion and the overreaction to life's struggles. In the midst of slavery, suffering, and war, she somehow manages to make everything all about her—*her* tragic losses, *her* epic love affairs, *her* heroic battles to save her beloved land. Completely self-absorbed and prone to sudden outbursts of emotion, we give Miss Scarlett the illustrious title of the textbook Disruptive Alpha.

The Disruptive Alpha suffers from a near-constant need for attention that drives her to do almost anything to secure her share of the spotlight and claim her rightful place at center stage. Notoriously self-centered, this Alpha female can be loud, disrespectful, abrasive, and dramatic. She simply isn't satisfied unless all eyes are on her and she is the topic of every conversation. Even with her mouth shut her presence can be overwhelming, and when she speaks she has a tendency to talk at and over people, rather than with them or to them.

Even if the Disruptive Alpha's ideas are good (and they often are), she presents them in a way that is anywhere from mildly off-putting to blatantly offensive, which usually closes her audience's ears. Like the obnoxious kid doing cannonballs in the pool while you're quietly trying to read, her boisterous, unruly, and intrusive energy is distracting— not to mention downright annoying—and her domineering personality leaves little room for anyone else to voice his or her point of view.

This Alpha, a master at creating tension and discord, may try to simply stir the pot by bringing up provocative subjects with which she knows others will disagree. She may also make an inflammatory comment at just the right moment or share a juicy bit of gossip that sends her listeners reeling. There is no mistaking the moment a Disruptive Alpha enters a room because the mood instantly changes from peaceful and calm to chaotic and combative.

The woman who wields Disruptive Alpha energy is quite fond of exaggerating minor details. Little setbacks escalate into explosive outbursts; even a drop of spilled coffee or a missed freeway exit can be cause for hysterics. This Alpha's only reaction is overreaction. The Disruptive Alpha is like an egocentric child: she feels what happens to her is all that matters and she doesn't understand that other people exist, too. Her attention-seeking behavior may express itself in any number of ways, from throwing tantrums, to spreading rumors, or playing the victim until her "woe is me" story has monopolized everyone's minds and emotions. There is only one thing this diva loves more than a good scandal, and that's spreading it like wildfire until everyone has been sucked into her dramatic tale.

On the upside, the Disruptive Alpha can be tons of fun to be around—occasionally and in small doses, that is. Her love of attention means there is rarely a dull moment and the fact that she always has a story to tell definitely keeps things interesting. This girl makes an excellent workout buddy—her theatrics will keep your mind off the steep hill you're climbing on the treadmill or the number of repetitions you're cranking out on the abdominal machine. Hey, who doesn't enjoy a good soap opera every now and then? And as long as her faithful viewers keep tuning in, the star of the show is likely to remain relatively tame and happy.

The Dark Side of the Drama Queen

There is, however, one glitch in the Disruptive Alpha's behavior: because she has a tendency to carelessly run others over with both her words and her deeds, she is often left performing her grand monologues to an empty theater. Sure, she may dominate the stage for a moment, but over time she loses

The Disruptive Alpha is like a tornado that tears through a city, oblivious to both the effect she has on others and the destruction she leaves behind in her wake.

the attention and admiration of her audience because no one enjoys being endlessly interrupted or overshadowed. The Disruptive Alpha is like a tornado that tears through a city, oblivious to both the effect she has on others and the destruction she leaves behind in her wake.

The Disruptive Alpha in the Workplace

Professionally, the Disruptive Alpha's addiction to drama takes her attention away from getting the success she wants. No one can dispute that she knows how to create a flurry of activity, but nothing new or truly genius can transpire because she's not nearly as interested in succeeding as she is in being seen. Her productivity and focus are held hostage by her neediness, blocking her from moving forward while keeping her stuck repeating the same old dramas. Co-workers may fear confronting her or offering helpful advice because she often handles constructive criticism by lashing out defensively, making them look like the bad guys who are out to get her. (Rest assured she will probably exaggerate the incident and tell the rest of the office she was verbally attacked.) Office mates quickly learn to sidestep the landmines that she creates, or they'll be the ones left to defuse the bomb.

The Disruptive Alpha's antics can pull an entire company off track; no one can stay on topic because she is forever bringing the focus back to herself. And while most people won't be able to pinpoint the exact cause of the distraction, someone who understands the underlying motivations of the Disruptive Alpha can spot her tactics a mile away. A few years ago, while attending a weekend business retreat, Christy was able to do just that.

Like most of my colleagues who were invited to attend our annual retreat, I arrived on Friday morning and was immediately impressed not only by how smoothly the logistics were handled, but also by how much I enjoyed participating in the sessions themselves. We were exposed to loads of new information but because the group was so cohesive, we were able to assimilate the concepts quickly and even managed to have a good time doing it.

When the conference resumed the following Saturday morning, we were joined by a coworker, Anna, who had not been in attendance on Friday. Now, most people who arrived late to a business meeting that was already in progress would probably decide to do a little more listening than talking in order to get up to speed on what was being discussed. Ah, but what would seem the logical choice to most people is completely counterintuitive to the Disruptive Alpha! Not only was Anna unable to harmonize with the group synergy that had been created the day before, she seemed determined to obliterate it. Virtually every point the presenter made was met with a comment by Anna, whose interruptions seemed to serve no other purpose than trying to make everyone aware of how smart, special, and uniquely important she was.

Eventually, her constant disruptions knocked the guest speaker off his game and he was unable to deliver his presentation in the same fluid and inspired way he had done just a day earlier. In addition, those who had come to the conference to learn something new from someone with valuable experience grew annoyed and even infuriated by Anna's repeated pleas for attention. The atmosphere in the room quickly deteriorated, and I watched in amazement as the majority of the conference attendees spiraled away from feeling creative and energetic to irritated and disinterested, simply because they were unable to concentrate on the information that was being presented.

Yes, she succeeded at capturing the attention of everyone in the room, including the presenter, and ensured that all eyes were on her. And while this no doubt made her feel important at that *moment*, her behavior on that *day* ultimately damaged her reputation and her career.

* * *

Working in harmony with others in the office may take some getting used to, especially for the Disruptive Alpha who is in the habit of hijacking the attention of everyone around her. But as you learn to cultivate a calm and balanced work environment, you will see your creativity rise as well as your productivity. Respect and harmony begin to flourish where chaos and confusion once dominated. No longer distracted by the unending drama of workplace conflict, you find that you have the focus and energy to invest in designing the prosperous career you deserve.

> ### Bitch Tips for the Disruptive Alpha at Work
>
> Think about a shotgun that scatters its impact in a hundred different directions; then think of a single-barrel pistol that directs all of its power toward one specific target. This image may help you to remember that you can be so much more productive when your energy is calm rather than chaotic, focused rather than frazzled. Slow down, get centered, and consciously create a work environment that is balanced and harmonious. From this place of tranquility you open the floodgates for creative genius to flow!

The Disruptive Alpha in Relationships

Take a peek into the private life of the Disruptive Alpha and you'll discover that her intimate relationships often suffer from a lack of genuine connection as well as reciprocity. Her own point of reference is sometimes all she can see—*her* needs, *her* wants, and *her* feelings. Seldom (if ever) does she think about her partner's needs or wants, his interests or concerns. To put it mildly, the Disruptive Alpha is high maintenance, and being around her can be emotionally and physically exhausting.

It's not long before her spouse or significant other tires of the drama. Even the cutest gal loses her appeal when her guy has to deal with the constant fallout of her emotions.

Her theatrics and melodrama overshadow his needs, and over time he may long for a more serene woman who takes a legitimate interest in him and desires a more peaceful, meaningful connection. On the other hand, if he is truly in love with her (or addicted to the drama she creates), he may indulge her egocentric ways and walk on eggshells to avoid making himself the target of her tantrums.

A relationship that is filled with turmoil and conflict is neither healthy nor satisfying. Although the Disruptive Alpha is comfortable in chaos—or even *thrives* on it—her partner may not be. Her high-strung, overly sensitive personality, combined with her addiction to drama, may just send him packing. If she can learn to tone down the drama and make room for him to express himself, she will find that the relationship flourishes. And the more he feels seen and valued by her, the more he will want to give back, organically and without provocation.

Bitch Tips for the Disruptive Alpha Partner

Share the spotlight with your mate. For every question or two he asks about you, ask something about him. By taking a genuine interest in him—his career, his hobbies, and his passions—you cultivate a deeper level of intimacy and a more fulfilling relationship. And who knows, you might even find it refreshing to step out of your own world and into his every once in a while!

The Disruptive Alpha as a Mother

Of all the Alpha types, the Disruptive Alpha is the least likely to become a mother, maybe because she intuitively senses that having children would deflect some of the attention that she craves for herself. If she does choose motherhood (by blood or by marriage), chances are high that she will treat her children more like accessories than important, valuable human beings with needs and desires of their own. In her presence, they may feel unseen or unheard, as she tends to steal attention from them. As her children get older and life's spotlight eventually lands on them, this "drama mama" may unconsciously find a way to make their accomplishments about her. Their high school graduation parties become outlets for her to seek acknowledgement for her latest achievement at work. Their dance recitals turn into the perfect events for her to work through the ugly argument she had with her husband. Oh, and dinnertime is often the ideal platform from which to vent her many grievances and injustices. In the end, her children either learn how to outdo her in order to get noticed—or worse, they simply fade into the background, feeling too insignificant to be seen.

> *As her children get older and life's spotlight eventually lands on them, this "drama mama" may unconsciously find a way to make their accomplishments about her.*

Upstaging our children or overreacting to the smallest mishaps isn't good for them, nor does it build trust in the relationship as a whole. They're more likely to share their ups and downs with us if they can count on us to remain calm—or at least try. Even though our initial impulse may be to freak out in true drama mama fashion, our kids benefit more from a composed demeanor and will be more likely to turn to us in the future for guidance.

By taking a genuine interest in their lives (which means putting our oh-so-important agenda on the back burner from time to time), we let our kids know how valuable and significant they are. Taking time out from our ever-consuming dramas to focus on our children is vital for their growth and development, and it's a nice break for us, too.

Bitch Tips for the Drama Mama

At least a few times a week, make it all about them! Take an interest in their friends, their hobbies, and their schoolwork. If they love to dance, ask them to show you their latest dance moves. If they're into skateboarding, go with them to the local skate park and watch them master the half pipe. (Just remember, you're there to *watch*, not to make a scene.)

The Disruptive Alpha as a Friend

Since everything in the Disruptive Alpha's universe revolves around her, she has little attention left over to invest in the interests or happenings of anyone else, and as a result her friends often wind up feeling unseen and unimportant. Being a member of her entourage (with its constant flurry of activity) has appeal in the beginning, but in the absence of respect and intimacy, her "peeps" eventually choose to opt out. The constant waterworks and endless obsessing over the details of her life make her draining to be around. Her inability to control her emotions wears thin as she causes embarrassing scenes in restaurants over small incidents, blows minor offenses into major fouls, starts nasty arguments over offhanded comments, throws tantrums, and launches tirades over insignificant everyday happenings. In the mind of the Disruptive Alpha, even the routine experience becomes larger than life, and she expects her friends to drop what they're doing and be as captivated with her as she is with herself.

If she shows up crying at your child's birthday party, you're expected to put the piñata on hold and rush to her side. (Six-year-olds won't have a problem with that, right?) Or when she calls at 3 A.M., intoxicated and confused, you are expected to hop in your car and go find her (after all, sleep is highly overrated). In the Disruptive Alpha's world, her crisis is your crisis and her problems are your top priority. And that means *her* needs overshadow yours, hands down!

When we cross the line into Disruptive Alpha behavior, we become self-absorbed, burdening our girlfriends with all of our problems and draining intimacy from the relationship. Of course, if our friends have good boundaries they won't play into our tragedies. They'll ignore our middle-of-the-night calls, let us know when we're monopolizing the conversation, and walk away before watching us make a scene. If we respect these boundaries, we may just keep these women as friends. But when our inner drama queen has a few more lines to deliver in her melodrama, our fed-up girlfriends may leave before the finale. Even the best of friends eventually tire of the one-sided friendship and the never-ending conflict, and will seek the company of gals who give as much as they get and enjoy the sounds of silence.

Bitch Tip for the Disruptive Alpha Friend

Before impulsively reaching out to your friends when the smallest mishaps occur, take a moment to breathe and collect your thoughts. Decide whether the situation is deserving of your time and energy, and whether it's worth the imposition on your friends. Life is filled with moments of conflict and uncertainty; learning to deal with them calmly and appropriately is the key to empowerment.

Wondering whether you might be a bit of a diva yourself? We all have a little Scarlett O'Hara in us, and the first step to change is always recognition. So check out the quiz below and see where you rank.

THE DISRUPTIVE DRAMA QUEEN—ARE YOU THIS TYPE OF ALPHA BITCH?

1. *You're the last to arrive at a dinner party and as you enter the room, everyone is happily engaged in conversation. You ...*

   A   Greet the people whose eyes meet yours and eventually make your way around the room.
   B   Tell at least three different people the details of the life drama that made you late.
   C   Announce your presence so loudly that everyone has to stop what they're doing to acknowledge you.
   D   Revel in the moment. After all, you arrived fashionably late on purpose so all eyes would be on you!

2. *You just received an honorable mention for a project you completed at work. You are more likely to ...*

   A   Email it to your entire list of family and friends; after all, news like this should be shared with others.
   B   Share the news in as grand a fashion as possible so you can bask in all the limelight you deserve.
   C   Tell your family and closest friends about your accomplishment and give them details if they ask.
   D   Go out of your way to "bump into" certain people, just so you can drop the bomb.

continued on next page ...

continued ...

3. *After finally making the decision to have a little cosmetic surgery, you ...*

A   Bring up the subject whenever possible and relish in your friends' jealousy or wait for them to tell you that "you are too pretty to ever need plastic surgery!"

B   Organize a phone tree so the minute you're out of surgery everyone will know how it went. You're sure they'll be on pins and needles.

C   Use the weeks leading up to the big event as an opportunity to show everyone the body part(s) in question.

D   Save your questions, concerns, elation, and excitement for your next doctor's appointment.

4. *Over a holiday dinner, your sister-in-law begins sharing the story of their recent remodel, and since you went through a similar experience not too long ago, you ...*

A   Nod and empathize. Those things never go as planned.

B   Pretend like you're listening while inside you're saying, "You think *that's* bad ... "

C   Give her a chance to finish her story and then promptly upstage her with your own.

D   Decide that one contractor saga is probably more than enough for the evening and wait to compare notes later on.

5. *Your husband happened to be at the right place at the right time and did something that helped a stranger in a time of need. After hearing about this, you ...*

A   Tell close friends and family members what happened, feeling a mixture of humility and pride.

B   Insist on proposing a toast to his heroism at the next twelve social functions you attend.

C   Share the story with anyone who seems to be interested and embellish it just a little each time.

D   Acknowledge him for his generous spirit and let him decide if
    and with whom he wants to share his experience.

6. *While listening to the radio on your drive into work, you win tickets
    to an upcoming concert. When you get to work, you . . .*

A   Barge into the office with "You won't believe what just
    happened!" and waste twenty minutes of company time while
    everyone tries to guess.
B   Call ten of your closest friends to share the news, making sure
    that everyone within earshot can hear you.
C   Tuck that little goodie into your back pocket and get to work.
D   Rack your brain to come up with ways to use the tickets as
    leverage.

7. *You get a flat tire on your way to an elegant black-tie affair. Clad in
    a gorgeous dress and heels, you . . .*

A   Handle the situation like any grown woman: inform the hostess
    of your late arrival and wait for the service truck to arrive.
B   Get out of your car to call the service truck—there's no way
    you're going to miss out on the opportunity to bask in all that
    male attention!
C   Change the tire yourself and ask a passerby to take pictures so
    you can upload them to your Facebook page later that evening.
D   Call a minimum of three friends to lament your "poor me" story.

8. *You happen to overhear a juicy bit of gossip shared by two coworkers
    who thought they were alone in the bathroom. You . . .*

A   Relay it directly to the person they were talking about, so she
    can confront her antagonists and clear her name.
B   Invite the person in question out to lunch and do your best to
    get the dish directly.
C   Immediately pass it on, regardless of whether it's true or not.
    Everyone loves an office scandal!

continued on next page . . .

continued...

D Enjoy the sensation you get from letting everyone know you have information they want before finally letting the cat out of the bag.

9. *When a close friend invites you to be a bridesmaid in her upcoming wedding, you...*

A Feel honored and share your friend's wish to make it the best day of her life.

B Can't believe she didn't ask you to be her maid of honor, but you'll get over it—or at least try.

C Are very excited. You love a good wedding, especially when you're center stage.

D Immediately start talking about the dress—yours, of course, not hers!

10. *You walk into your favorite coffee shop and see two of your friends sitting at a table. As you make your way over to say hello, you notice that they're in the middle of what looks like a pretty serious conversation. You...*

A Pull up a chair and launch into the horrendous fight you just had with your husband—after all, that's what friends are for, right?

B Say a quick "hey" and go about ordering your coffee.

C Have no idea what they were talking about so you call a few mutual friends to start venturing a guess.

D Give them a disgusted look and turn the other way. Obviously they were talking about you!

SCORING KEY:

1. a-1, b-3, c-5, d-4 • 2. a-3, b-5, c-1, d-4 • 3. a-5, b-3, c-4, d-1 • 4. a-1, b-3, c-5, d-2 • 5. a-2, b-5, c-4, d-1 • 6. a-5, b-4, c-1, d-3 • 7. a-1, b-3, c-5, d-4 • 8. a-2, b-3, c-4, d-5 • 9. a-1, b-3, c-4, d-5 • 10. a-5, b-1, c-3, d-4

ASSESSMENT:

Using the number that corresponds to each answer you gave, add up the total number of points.

If you scored 20 or fewer points, congratulations! You have successfully sidestepped most of the downfalls of the Disruptive Alpha Bitch.

If you scored between 21 and 35 points, chances are good that your life often feels like it's spinning in all directions. You might even be hearing complaints from friends and colleagues alike about your constant dramas and tantrums.

If you scored between 35 and 50 points, your addiction to drama is very likely draining you of resources that could further your career and bring you the personal fulfillment you desire. Chaos may provide a short-lived burst of excitement, but shifting your energy from disruptive and rude to balanced and harmonious will improve your relationships and bring you long-term fulfillment. This chapter will lead the way.

When we find ourselves slipping into disrespectful Disruptive Alpha behaviors, we must learn to take this as a sign that we are feeling underappreciated and undernourished, and in desperate need of our own attention. If we don't fill our self-love tanks, we put ourselves at risk for a collision down the road.

A Disturbance in the Force

In any area of our lives where we feel insignificant—whether in the success of our careers, the shape of our

bodies, or the strength of our family and personal relationships—we will be tempted to overcompensate by making
ourselves the center of attention, no matter what it takes to
get there. When we feel empty, our worst fear is that others
will ignore us, thereby confirming our hidden belief that we
are without value. When we fail to validate ourselves from
within, we seek that valida-
tion from outside sources in
order to feel significant and
special. We also begin to
look for other ways to make
ourselves happy—shopping,
eating, and drinking may
become ways the Disrupting
Alpha tries to comfort herself
if her latest antics didn't get
her the attention she wanted. Our need to be noticed by
those around us is so great that we persist in our attention-
seeking ways, even if we end up making fools of ourselves
or create animosity in the process. We're like toddlers when
we're in this frame of mind; we'd rather settle for negative
attention than receive no attention at all.

We're like toddlers when we're in this frame of mind; we'd rather settle for negative attention than receive no attention at all.

We disrupt the peace around us not only in an attempt
to make ourselves feel significant but also to distract ourselves from our own insecurities. Making mountains out of
molehills and maintaining an environment of constant drama ensures that we'll never have to confront the bigger issues brought about by our fears, shortcomings, and feelings
of inadequacy. The disruptions we create may temporarily
relieve us of feeling these painful emotions, but at a great

cost to our own happiness and personal fulfillment. Operating in this mode is like having access to only two channels on our emotional dial—stressed and hyperstressed. Because we are so accustomed to chaos, we wouldn't know what to do with ourselves if things came easily; unfortunately, most of the time they don't.

Drama and conflict create chaos and agitation in our lives, making it difficult to fulfill our desires smoothly or to connect with ourselves deeply enough to know what it is we really want. Imagine trying to steer a boat across an ocean when the water is choppy and waves are crashing all around. The turbulence would not only prevent you from reaching your destination but it could actually keep you from knowing where you are in relation to where you're trying to go. But if the sea were calm and glassy, your destination would be easier to reach, and the journey would be so much more enjoyable. This kind of smooth sailing is exactly what we experience when we shift our energetic stance from one that is disruptive and dramatic to one that is balanced and harmonious. In the same way that hysteria breeds more hysteria, the harmony in our lives increases when we intentionally and deliberately seek balance.

The Law of Balance and Harmony

The Law of Balance and Harmony asserts that by consciously choosing to align yourself with peaceful and tranquil energies, the floodgates of abundance open wide, providing you access to all the resources, wisdom, and blessings that life has to offer. This effortless state of being is achieved when you intend to harmonize with (rather than oppose) the people and circumstances around you. The more practiced you become at sidestepping drama and resting instead in tranquility, the easier it is to navigate through stormy waters.

In music, harmony is achieved when two or more notes merge into resonance—when they work together in symphony rather than compete to be the loudest. In life, we achieve harmony by seeking common ground between two or more people, ideas, or interests.

Infusing your life with harmonious energy is as simple as making the choice to slow down and leave the drama behind. Balanced thoughts are not harried—they're calm and focused, and therefore very potent. One action born from a mindset of tranquility is more powerful than a hundred that are driven by chaos. Why? Because, energetically speaking, harmonious forces are created through integration and purpose, while the force of disruption is scattered. You'll attract greater success and abundance into your life from a vibration of calm tranquility because your attention and resources won't be wasted on the irrelevant issues. By eliminating drama, an enormous amount of energy can be redirected to achieving goals and creating more fulfilling relationships.

In life, we achieve harmony by seeking common ground between two or more people, ideas, or interests.

For starters, a foundation of calm draws people in rather than pushing them away, which invites deeper connections and greater intimacy while vastly improving your relationships. Communication with others becomes more clear and direct and doesn't get lost in all the static that disruption breeds. Your partner has the freedom to step out of the shadows and contribute more because he's no longer just playing a supporting role in your drama. There is more peace in your family because others have room to express themselves. While at work you feel more focused and productive because your energy is not wasted away on silly things.

One action born from a mindset of tranquility is more powerful than a hundred that are driven by chaos.

Here are some tips to help you minimize the drama in your life:

- Change your words. Inflammatory words and phrases like "never," "always," and, "Oh, my god!" only add fuel to an already blazing fire. If you tone down your words, you will notice that your emotions will calm down, too.

- When you feel the Disruptive Alpha within about to appear, take a quick reality check. Is your life really going to end if he doesn't call? Will you never be employed again if your boss is disappointed in your work? Doing this will help to diffuse the habit of "catastrophic thinking" by applying a little logic to the situation.

- Identify the triggers that prompt you to over-react. Write down any patterns you notice and brainstorm ways you can sidestep them.

- Try to identify the payoff you receive by "freaking out." Is it stress relief or a quick rush of power or significance? Once you know what you get from these emotional outbursts, see if you can think of a better way to meet these needs.

- Don't assume and try not to jump to conclusions. Ask yourself if there is another way to look at the situation, or a logical reason for the other person's behavior. Snap judgments (as right as they may feel in the moment) often lead you down the wrong path and pull you away from your center.

When your Disruptive Alpha is running the show, the constant inner clamor can be so deafening that it's difficult to hear the voice of reason. By activating the Law of Balance and Harmony, you learn to see through the drama to more rational reactions and answers, which (as the following chart demonstrates) leads to a more positive path and far more rewarding outcomes.

	When Operating from a Disruptive Mindset	When Embracing Harmony and Balance
How We Perceive Life	• The world is my stage • Filled with upheaval and conflict, struggle and hardship	• There is enough attention and affection for everyone • Easy and fluid • Daily living is balanced and calm
How We Perceive Others	• Rivals who take my spotlight • Audience members	• Accepting of others • Equally important • United, not opposing others
How Others Perceive Us	• A drama queen • Manipulative and exploitive • Combative • Gossipy and backstabbing • Full of conflict and chaos • Attention seeker	• Calm • Relaxed • Open • Centered • Balanced
How We Feel	• Invisible and insignificant • Chaotic • Stressed • Insecure	• Relaxed • Peaceful and serene • Accepting • Balanced • Deeply connected to others

A woman who is calm and empowered does not need to seek outside attention for validation of her own worth. The attention she receives from others merely amplifies what she already gets from within. And when she's noticed, it's for her achievements, not the manipulative tactics she employs to be the center of attention. She is self-generating and therefore unstoppable.

Tranquility: The Key to Activating the Law of Balance and Harmony

As a woman who is both calm and empowered, you have access to the full range of your emotions; unlike the Disruptive Alpha, you understand how to express them artfully and without hysteria. You don't feel toppled over by the ups and downs of life, but instead have the ability to remain centered and calm regardless of what is happening around you. Consciously inviting calmness and tranquility into your life enables you to magnetize the ease and abundance you deserve. Tranquility is a potent field of energy from which to create; from a quiet and peaceful state, you can call forth all the blessings that the universe makes available to you in every moment.

When you find yourself in a difficult situation, or around a challenging person, and you feel your center of gravity shifting from centered and strong to shaky and turbulent, remember that you have a choice. You can give in to the habits and hysteria of the drama queen or you can align yourself with the authority and strength of true Feminine Power. The decision is yours to either impulsively react to the ups and downs of life, which diffuses your power, or infuse yourself with the energies of balance and harmony.

Here's a little visual to help solidify this concept...

Imagine yourself on the surface of the ocean where the waters are choppy and rough. Now see yourself slowly drifting down deep below the chaotic surface. Feel how quiet and still it gets the further down you go. You may be aware of the movement and turmoil above you, but you are removed from it—you are resting in a more tranquil and peaceful setting.

Seemingly unsolvable situations miraculously become solvable when you replace chaos and confusion with peace and calm. Rebecca had this experience herself, while flying across the country after cofacilitating a weekend conference.

On my return trip home from our last Goddess Retreat, I was booked on a small connecting flight out of Rochester, New York, that would take me to Chicago where I would catch a direct flight back to San Francisco. I arrived at the airport, checked in, and sat in the waiting area until it was time to board the plane. A few minutes later, it was announced over the PA that the connecting flight would be arriving late. Audible groans and caustic complaints reverberated through the waiting area as impatient travelers grasped the potential consequences of this delay. Chicago was the main hub from which each of us would be dispatched to our various destinations. Some were headed to Los Angeles; others to Las Vegas; a couple of young businessmen were on their way to Dubai. With every minute that ticked by, the tension escalated as people realized that their connecting flights might very well be leaving Chicago without them on board. Many waiting passengers—male and female—launched into disrespectful Disruptive Alpha mode, demanding that their needs be considered while demeaning the poor airline employees, who were powerless to do anything about the situation.

I have to admit that in the presence of all that stress, my inner Disruptive Alpha began to snarl. After all, my connecting flight back to the Bay Area left me only an hour to change planes. Fortunately, though, I had just spent an incredible weekend soaking up the high, harmonious vibrations of the Goddess Retreat and was completely dialed in to the power of tranquility. While the other passengers paced the terminal—guzzling coffee, complaining to one another, and frantically trying to reach people on their cell phones—I took a deep breath and attuned my energy to those of tranquility and calm, knowing that these forces are infinitely more powerful than disruption and disrespect. We boarded the plane an hour late and were scheduled to land in Chicago at 11:50 A.M., the exact time that my connecting flight was scheduled to take off.

Needless to say, the in-flight atmosphere was far from serene. You could almost hear people thinking, *"Fly faster! I have a flight to catch!"* When we finally landed in Chicago, we were again delayed because of a faulty door that wouldn't open. Angry passengers pushed and shoved their way toward the front of the plane as crew members tried to fix the door. From the tiny windows of our plane, we watched as one jumbo jet after another pushed back, leaving everyone to wonder if that was their connecting flight to Los Angeles or Dubai, or mine to San Francisco.

I remained in my seat, aligning my thoughts and emotions with the feminine forces of calm—trusting that this energy would serve me.

When we were finally free to go, I sailed through the Jetway and before I could even consult the flight board to see which gate I was supposed to report to, I heard my name being called over the PA, directing me to my new gate. Perfect! I was halfway to my gate when a flight attendant rushed toward me and asked, "San Francisco?" "Yes," I replied, and she said, "This way. Let me take your bag." Not only did she escort me to my flight, she gave me a helping hand with my luggage! I boarded the plane and had just sat down as the jet pushed back on the tarmac.

> *On the flight home I reflected on the countless details that had come together in order for this outcome to unfold and realized that if I had allowed anger, conflict, or disharmony to disrupt my energy, the outcome would have been vastly different.*

On the flight home I reflected on the countless details that had come together in order for this outcome to unfold and realized that if I had allowed anger, conflict, or disharmony to disrupt my energy, the outcome would have been vastly different. By aligning myself with the forces of tranquility and calm, the universe did the work for me and miracles unfolded on their own.

* * *

Establishing an inner foundation of tranquility nourishes us on all levels—physically, emotionally, and spiritually. By choosing to withdraw from the conflict and confusion of the inner drama queen and aligning our energies with those of balance and harmony, our vibrations shift from turbulent and chaotic to calm, clear, and harmonious.

Here are some practical suggestions for making this shift:

- Take time every day just for you. Use this time to unplug and relax. Linger in a warm bath or enjoy a soothing cup of tea. Read a good novel. This is your time to unwind, de-compress, and soak in some much-needed peace and quiet.

- Try yoga. Even beginners report feeling less stressed and more relaxed after their first class. Look for classes that incorporate medi-tation to quiet the "mind chatter" and pro-mote inner peace.

- Listen to relaxing music. Music can have a powerfully calming effect. Get in the habit of turning off the television and putting on some beautiful music. Before long you'll feel yourself "vibing" to the soothing tunes!

- Visit www.tamingyouralphabitch.com and download a guided meditation on pure potentiality, allowing, oneness, tranquility, or abundance.

Feminine energy is quiet and potent, not disruptive and boisterous. By tapping into the feminine principles of calmness and tranquility—centering yourself around the knowledge that overreacting just adds to the chaos—you engage the Law of Harmony and Balance, which makes stress fade, drama disappear, and life easier. Because your energy is not wasted on disrespecting, disrupting, or upstaging anyone else, the results you seek are magnetically drawn to you. The exercise that follows will support you in tapping into this magical state.

EXERCISE
Transforming Disruption into Harmony

Set aside twenty to thirty minutes of uninterrupted time to complete this exercise. Make sure that you have a journal or a piece of paper and pen nearby to record any insights or actions that may arise.

To begin, allow yourself to recall a recent experience when you actually caught yourself in the act of being disruptive or combative. It might have been at work, with friends or family, or in your relationship with your husband or children. See if you can replay it as if it were happening in this moment. As vividly as you can, picture the people involved in the situation and the circumstances that led up to it. What were you saying or doing? How did others react? Imagine that you had the ability to step outside of yourself, and observe your behavior as others do. What would you see? Write down whatever details you can recall.

Remembering that all disruptive behaviors are driven by fear and insecurity, see if you can recall what you were feeling in that moment. Give yourself permission to be vulnerable; recognize the underlying fears and doubts that caused you to feel that disruptive behaviors were your only option. Ask yourself, "What was I afraid of?" and allow yourself to hear whatever answer arises. How much of your energy is sucked out of you when you're engaged in conflict or chaos? Let yourself feel the emotional toll that drama takes on your body and mind.

Now let yourself hear the thoughts that triggered these emotions. Give yourself time to listen deeply and write down as many as you can identify.

Going deeper, allow yourself to move beyond your thoughts to the core belief that ignited this thinking within you. Be patient, simply allowing the belief to reveal itself in perfect time. As you uncover your limiting belief about yourself, others, and life, notice how you feel when you hold this belief in your awareness. Does it make you feel scared, vulnerable, or insignificant? Describe how you feel when you hold this limiting belief as the truth.

Ask yourself what new belief you could affirm that would support you in creating more ease and harmony in your life. Try these on and see how they feel:

* *I create peace and harmony in all aspects of my life.*
* *I am seen and valued for who I am, not for my dramatics.*
* *I choose peace and tranquility throughout my day.*
* *I remain calm and centered in the midst of all circumstances of my life.*

As you identify a new, more empowering belief, write it down in your journal and allow it to become deeply anchored in your consciousness by saying it a few times out loud. Fully embody the meaning of this statement.

Now ask yourself what actions you could take—right now or in the future—to meet your needs for recognition or validation. Could you spend a little time each day focusing on your positive qualities and inner beauty? Could you take a walk in nature and absorb the tranquility that surrounds you? Write down whatever ideas come to you. Allow yourself to feel the way you would feel if you actually took those actions. Would you feel more serene? More balanced?

With your next breath, consciously and deliberately release any thoughts or feelings that lead to inner discord, and allow yourself to feel calm and centered as you reaffirm your new belief.

Make a commitment to remind yourself of this new empowering belief several times throughout your day, each time immersing yourself deeper into the truth of the statement.

Take a moment to savor this feeling.

• • • • • • • • • • • • • •

Go to www.alphabitchbook.com to download an additional meditation on living in balance and harmony, and use the authorization code TYABFREE.

Bitch Tip

Feeling the urge to steal another's limelight or force your way to center stage? Remember that peace is far more powerful than discord. Don't play into whatever drama is unfolding and decide instead to purposefully choose tranquility. A calm mind and body allow you to more easily return to your innate feminine state. When you are in balance and harmony, you are perfectly aligned to attract your greatest desires.

chapter five

The Driving Force behind All Alpha Behaviors

A s we've seen, the desperation to attain validation, security, self-esteem, attention, or a higher social status from an outside source can awaken the Alpha Bitch within any of us, and once the fangs come out, the consequences to ourselves and those around us can be devastating.

By now it's probably clear that the underlying state of mind that drives all four Alpha Bitch types to such imbalanced and aggressive extremes is not one of confidence or self-assuredness but one of insecurity and insufficiency. The Forceful Alpha uses bullying and intimidation, the Controlling Alpha becomes overbearing and micromanaging, the Competitive Alpha can be relentless and underhanded, and the Disruptive Alpha resorts to attention-seeking behaviors. However our inner Alpha Bitch reveals herself—whether as forceful, controlling, competitive, or attention-seeking—it is vital to understand that these behaviors are *always* triggered by the core beliefs of lack and insufficiency, which send us spiraling into panic and fear. Like our neighbor's high-strung Chihuahua straining at the end of her leash, we move through our lives yapping and snapping at every shadow, bringing conflict and anxiety with us wherever we go.

Fear and insufficiency bring out the aggression in the Forceful Alpha, compelling her to push harder and exert more effort—to fight for everything and to dominate others in the process. The Forceful Alpha operates from a state of *perpetual dissatisfaction*, a constant need for more. She's afraid that if she lets her guard down and appears vulnerable, others will take advantage of her. Or, if she's not aggressive and overbearing, she will never get the success and respect she deserves. Therefore, she is always striving for some goal that she thinks will bring her fulfillment. Because she is always trying to fill this inner hunger, she drives herself to exhaustion, constantly seeking "just this one more thing" that will (or she thinks it will) bring her lasting satisfaction.

However our inner Alpha Bitch reveals herself— whether as forceful, controlling, competitive, or attention-seeking—it is vital to understand that these behaviors are always triggered by the core beliefs of lack and insufficiency.

Fear and scarcity are the forces that drive the Controlling Alpha's internal operating system as well. Her point of reference is always focused on all the potential pitfalls of life. Because she doesn't look at life through a lens of sufficiency, she can't see all that is right with the world. Instead, she looks at life through a lens of insufficiency so she is always aware of all that could go wrong in the absence of her constant vigilance. She is afraid of what she doesn't know or can't control, so she makes sure she controls everything! In her life, there is always something that needs fixing or perfecting, and she believes that she is the only one who can do it. If she isn't overseeing everyone and everything, she feels uneasy, sometimes without even knowing why. Fear starts the engine that drives her constant anxiety and vigilance and soon catapults her into controlling all the people and events in her life.

From that same core belief of insufficient resources, the Competitive Alpha naturally views others as her rivals—poised and ready to take her share of the available men, job opportunities, or limelight. She relentlessly compares herself to her friends, coworkers, neighbors, and family members, turning them into enemies rather than allies and depriving herself of camaraderie and support in the process. A constant battle rages within her to get there first and then hold tight to the "win," because her limiting beliefs assure her that others are on her heels to take what is rightfully hers. Suspicion and defensiveness build a wall that separates her from any real relationships, leaving her feeling isolated and alone. Sure, she may have those brief moments of exhilaration when she captures a much sought-after objective—she lands a promotion or gets the last word in an argument with her husband—but almost before the victory dance in her head comes to an end, something else rises that she has to defeat. The Competitive Alpha is afraid that she may not be good enough, so she tries to be the best at everything.

The Disruptive Alpha's fear manifests as a perpetual feeling of emptiness. She screams for attention not because she feels whole and complete but because she is lacking the inner confidence of an empowered woman. She turns to anything that makes her feel better—including things that are bad for her, like a guy who mistreats her (hey, any attention is better than no attention), other Disruptive Alphas (they understand why she feels how she does), and even fatty foods (a girl needs something to help fill the internal void). Her dramas are fueled by the fear that unless all eyes are fixed on her, she will disappear completely. Without attention, positive or negative, she fears she will cease to exist. Within her is a void that she desperately tries to fill through the acknowledgment and attention that her theatrics bring.

Our underlying beliefs in lack and scarcity—the perception that there are simply not enough love, attention, money, or other resources to go around—raises our Alpha Bitch hackles, and provokes us to bare our teeth and fight for our fair share. In this lack-entrenched, fear-driven state, we react rather than respond, dominate rather than cooperate. In other words, we lash out unreasonably because we are afraid that we are not good enough to hold on to the limited resources that are available. Our preoccupation with what we *don't* have (or what we do, but could be taken away) makes us incredibly cutthroat, and we view almost everyone through the lens of, "What can she do for me?" or as an adversary who could take away what we do have.

Living 24/7 in the mindset of insufficiency—as most Alphas do—locks us into perpetual fight-or-flight mode. We're so focused on what we must do to *survive* that we can't even imagine how it would feel to relax and *thrive*. And our underlying allegiance to limitation ensures that we'll continue to experience lack, if not as actual material poverty, then as a shortage of love, happiness, time, or peace of mind.

Limitation and insufficiency drive us to act out all Alpha Bitch behaviors. Some are overt and hostile, others are quietly manipulative, but all of them take us away from our true source of power by tempting us to look outside ourselves for validation of our inner worth and convincing us that the only way we can win is if someone else loses.

You see, no matter how much love, success, or material abundance we already have, our underlying beliefs of lack and limitation skew our worldview, preventing us from receiving the blessings that are all around us and keeping us stuck in a constant state of dissatisfaction. We might have just returned from a fabulous cruise, but when we're operating from lack, all we can think about is that we didn't get the room with the veranda ... and our best friend did. We miss out on the sweet moments with our kids because we're fixated on their less-than-perfect grade point averages. Or we feel resentful when they ask their dad for answers, because all we can think about is that they love him more than us. We disregard our husband's kind gestures because our attention naturally lands on what he *didn't* do—the lawn that didn't get mowed, or his socks that never seem to make it into the laundry basket. Of course, we also fail to acknowledge our own inner attributes; they're usually overshadowed by our perceived faults and failings.

The same critical internal voice that continuously points out our flaws sends us a very damaging message: who we are and what we have are simply not enough. The belief that we are somehow flawed and inadequate triggers thoughts of scarcity and evokes one of the most primitive and powerful emotions any human being is capable of feeling: raw, unadulterated fear. If you look closely at the obnoxious, snarling Chihuahua, you can see it shaking violently because underneath that seemingly tough bark, it's terrified.

Fuel for the Alpha Bitch Fire

Sure, we may try to conceal our anxiety by acting aloof or superior, or mask our insecurity by going out of our way to convince others of our importance, or hide behind comfort foods that put bandages over our emotional scars. However, if we're really honest with ourselves, we will see that all of our bragging, dramatizing, and order-barking comes from a place of weakness, not from strength; more often than not, our emotional state is one of frenzied panic, not the cool confidence we try to portray.

Fear and insufficiency are the sparks that ignite the primitive Alpha within each of us. These misguided notions keep us in a state of constant overdrive, because we believe that unless we are constantly on guard, we will miss out on something important. And without even realizing it, we project this fear into the future—collecting, analyzing, and focusing on all the factors that may lead to our inevitable downfall. We anticipate the worst possible outcome in virtually every situation and unwittingly become our own worst enemies.

If the boss calls us in for a meeting at work, we immediately think we're getting fired, not praised for our proficiency. We're sure our presentation will be judged as unacceptable instead of excellent. Or we're convinced that, once again, a coworker will be promoted ahead of us.

If our husbands go out of their way to invite us out to dinner, we can't help but envision the worst. "It must be a setup," we think to ourselves. "He's about to drop a bomb. Maybe he's been fired from his job or he lost all our savings in a bad investment or he's leaving me for a younger woman." It never occurs to us that he might just want to spend a lovely evening with his favorite person.

When a friend leaves a voice message saying she needs to talk right away, we immediately anticipate the worst— she must be moving across country or she's just been diagnosed with terminal brain cancer. It's not until she reveals her wedding plans that we breathe a sigh of relief—and that's assuming we're not the competitive type!

And when it comes to parenting, our fears go into overdrive. A note to call the school can only mean one thing: our sons have been expelled or our daughters were critically injured on the playground swings. How silly we feel when we find out that the teacher just needs a dozen cupcakes for the class party.

Of course, our fatalistic imagination only gives us more cause to panic and adds fuel to our already-raging Alpha Bitch fire. When caught up in the clutches of a limiting mindset, we can quickly spiral to "the dark side." To see how much of a hold fear and insufficiency have on you, take the quiz on the following page.

ARE YOU RULED BY FEAR AND INSUFFICIENCY?

1. *Your sister calls out of the blue. Your immediate thought is that she . . .*

    A   Is going to ask to borrow your favorite dress, along with the matching shoes and handbag, *and* your best earrings.

    B   Probably wants to invite you to lunch. It's been months since the two of you have seen one another.

    C   Wants your help in planning your parents' upcoming anniversary party.

    D   Is letting you know that her company is in trouble, and that her hours are being cut, along with her salary!

2. *You and a close single girlfriend are both ready to meet "Mr. Right." When she calls to tell you about a date that went exceptionally well, you feel . . .*

    A   Excited.

    B   Envious.

    C   Hopeful.

    D   Defeated.

3. *While shopping at your favorite store's semiannual sale, you see another woman making her way toward a one-of-a-kind pair of sandals on the clearance rack. You . . .*

    A   Pick up your step to beat her to the rack; they're probably the last pair in your size.

    B   Wait until she's done eyeing them before moving in for the kill.

    C   Concede the victory and, dejected, make your way to another department.

    D   Let her have them; there are plenty of others to choose from.

4. *At an office party, you notice a female coworker having an animated conversation with your boyfriend. You . . .*

    A   Make a beeline across the room and promptly break it up.

B   Smile confidently at your man and continue your own conversation.

C   Play it cool on the outside, despite the pit of anxiety in your stomach.

D   Invent an excuse to swipe your boyfriend from the clutches of that vixen.

5. *It's Sunday night and you have a huge week ahead, including a big presentation at work, a dinner party with friends, and an event you agreed to help organize at your child's school. You . . .*

A   Take charge. You start organizing and planning every last detail until the wee hours of the morning.

B   Kick your body into overdrive (and overwhelm); the adrenaline (and that high-calorie Frappuccino) is the only thing keeping you from dropping the ball.

C   Postpone your social plans until a less hectic week, trusting that your friends will understand.

D   Take a moment to appreciate your full and active life, and approach the week ahead with a feeling of gratitude.

6. *After finding out that the new carpet you ordered will not be installed before your in-laws arrive for a visit, you . . .*

A   Worry that they'll think you are a horrible housekeeper and settle for carpet that can be installed right away.

B   Shrug it off and comfort yourself with the thought that every stain has an interesting story to tell.

C   Wait for the carpet you wanted, but use credit to buy several large area rugs to put down while your in-laws are in town.

D   Demand that your in-laws change their travel plans so your house will be in tip-top shape for their visit.

7. *When you're asked to volunteer in a community service project at work, you . . .*

A   Jump at the chance to help those less fortunate than yourself while helping your company at the same time.

continued on next page . . .

continued…

B   Base your decision on whether your involvement will win you enough accolades to justify your time.

C   Decline, saying you'd love to help but you just don't think you can afford the time commitment.

D   Worry about what your coworkers will think if you decline and force yourself into doing it regardless of whether you want to or not.

8.   *After a college friend phones to tell you that he just got laid off from his job, you …*

A   Immediately schedule a meeting with your supervisor to make sure that your own job is secure.

B   Remind your friend of all the professional contacts he has, and brainstorm next steps for him to find an even better job.

C   Feel grateful that you have a job and feel a little more motivated to work hard to keep it.

D   Can't help but worry that the axe is going to fall on you next.

9.   *After years of searching, you finally meet a guy who is exciting and successful … and married. You …*

A   Walk away. There are plenty of great guys who are also available.

B   Have an affair with him; after all, a little male attention is better than none at all.

C   Are tempted to sell out your long-term desires for a bit of short-term gratification. Who knows when you'll get another opportunity like this one?

D   Identify the characteristics you find attractive in the married man and add them to the list of "must-have" qualities that you want your ultimate soul mate to possess.

10.   *When your neighbors return from their Mediterranean cruise gushing about their exotic adventures and luxurious accommodations, you …*

A   Can't help thinking how selfish they are to go on and on about their adventures when they know that you have never been out of the country.

B Feel utterly depressed. Barring some miracle, you'll never have the means to afford such an extravagant vacation.
C Cut the conversation short, making a mental note to avoid them until they've gotten over their postvacation glow.
D Remind yourself that if you have the desire to experience something, you also have the ability to create it.

SCORING KEY:

1. a-4, b-1, c-3, d-5 • 2. a-1, b-4, c-2, d-5 • 3. a-5, b-4, c-3, d-1 • 4. a-5, b-1, c-3, d-4 • 5. a-5, b-4, c-2, d-1 • 6. a-4, b-1, c-3, d-5 • 7. a-1, b-5, c-3, d-4 • 8. a-4, b-1, c-2, d-5 • 9. a-2, b-5, c-3, d-1 • 10. a-3, b-5, c-4, d-1

ASSESSMENT:

Using the number that corresponds to each answer you gave, add up the total number of points.

If you scored 20 or fewer points, relax. Your underlying problem is not fear.

If you scored between 21 and 35 points, there's a good chance that you're more driven by anxiety than you are motivated by possibility. Odds are good that you feel stressed out a majority of the time.

If you scored between 35 and 50 points, you are most likely keenly aware of everything that you don't have and may have even given up hope that you'll ever achieve the goals you hold dear. By shifting your reference point from what you lack to the abundance that is already yours, your anxiety will lessen and you'll become more receptive to the opportunities that are all around you. This chapter will show you how.

The Eternally "Half-Empty" Glass

Not only do our underlying beliefs in lack and limitation give rise to some pretty unbecoming personality traits, they also directly impact our ability to attract the abundance we desire. The circumstances in which we find ourselves—the ease of our relationships, the stability of our finances, and the degree of vitality we feel in our bodies—are always directly correlated to what we believe we are worthy of receiving. So naturally, if our mindset is consumed by thoughts of insufficiency—we are not enough, and there are not enough resources for us—we will continue to create and re-create the experience of lack.

Our beliefs are powerful determinants for future events, not only because they alter our behaviors but because they alter our energy.

To soften our hard Alpha edges and return to our natural feminine state of ease and grace, we must realize that every time we focus on what we don't have or worry about what *might* be taken away from us, we are using our energy to imagine a future that is anything but desirable! Our worries, fears, and beliefs in scarcity are seeds we plant for upcoming life experiences.

If we believe that there are insufficient resources available to fulfill everyone's needs, we will continually find evidence that supports this belief. This is what is known in psychology as the self-fulfilling prophecy—what you believe will happen often does, simply because you act in ways that cause the events to occur. For instance, if you believe that all men cheat, your actions toward your boyfriend may err on the side of distrustful and suspicious. You might question his every move or check up on his whereabouts, snoop through his emails, or pester him incessantly when he's out with his friends. These behaviors may eventually push him away, possibly into the arms of another woman, thereby confirming your belief that "all men cheat." Our beliefs are powerful determinants for future events, not only because they alter our behaviors but because they alter our *energy*.

With each thought of what's missing, wrong, or insufficient, we unwittingly shift our point of attraction by focusing on all that is missing, wrong, and insufficient. From this state of consciousness, the proverbial glass is always half empty and no matter what we have, it never feels like enough. Because we view the world through the lens of "insufficiency," both in the sense that we are not good enough and there is not enough for everyone, we panic and turn the reins over to our inner Alpha, which instantly diminishes our tranquility, as well as our effectiveness in the world.

Because we view the world through the lens of "insufficiency," both in the sense that we are not good enough and there is not enough for everyone, we panic and turn the reins over to our inner Alpha, which instantly diminishes our tranquility, as well as our effectiveness in the world.

The fact that dogs can sense fear in humans and react to it suggests that it's more than a fleeting emotion; fear is an energetic state of being that is registered by everyone and everything that comes in contact with it. When a woman who is entrenched in lack, insufficiency, and fear walks into a room, she brings this energy with her; even if she never utters a word, people pick up on this vibe and respond accordingly. They may instinctively feel the need to pacify her, walk on eggshells around her, or avoid her altogether. She may agitate others with her energy, provoking aggression or anxiety in them. The good news is that abundance also resides at a particular frequency, and when we attune ourselves to it, we tap into our innate ability to create the outcomes we desire without struggling, striving, or trying to force them to happen.

Until we release our belief in scarcity, we'll never fully allow abundance into our lives. Our limiting beliefs block us from accessing the greater levels of prosperity we want. So how can we release the thoughts that fuel our Alpha ways and deny us the lives we deserve? By tuning into our emotions. They will indicate whether our predominant thoughts are empowering or limiting. If we feel happy, hopeful, and uplifted, we can rest assured that we're on track and our thoughts are in alignment with our essential abundant nature. But if we're feeling anxious, angry, or desperate, it's time to do some energetic fine-tuning. Here's how.

Steps for Releasing Lack and Limitation

1. Consciously identify the beliefs that are holding you back. Choose a problematic area of your life and write down whatever insights or limiting beliefs come to mind. Don't judge or analyze the thoughts, just let them flow.

2. Once your subconscious mind reveals the negative beliefs you've been carrying, challenge them. Ask yourself whether these beliefs are really the truth or if they're just some things you inherited from your family, your upbringing, or your culture. As you contemplate the beliefs, notice whether they empower you by making you feel strong, or disempower you by undermining your confidence.

3. Anchor in a new belief by regularly affirming a more empowering thought. Henry David Thoreau tells us that "as a single footstep will not make a path on the earth, so a single thought will not make a pathway in the mind. To make a deep physical path, we walk again and again. To make a deep mental path, we must think over and over the kind of thoughts we wish to dominate our lives."[1] Repeat the more desirable thought often. Even if you don't fully believe it at first, over

[1] Henry David Thoreau, excerpt from his journals

time it will become your predominant way of thinking.

No matter how hard you work, you'll never earn the success you desire and deserve until you identify the limitations that have been keeping you from it. These limitations have nothing to do with your personal history or your perceived shortcomings; they are not the fault of other people who have more than you do, and they are certainly not due to any lack of resources in the universe. The only barrier that stands between you and the life of excellence that you envision in your heart and mind is an internal one—and this means that removing it is something only you can do. By activating the Law of Sufficiency and Abundance, you generate your desired outcomes quietly, easily, and through the sheer force of your magnetism—in true Feminine Power style.

The Law of Sufficiency and Abundance

This law operates according to the universal truth that we are all born whole and complete, sufficient, and abundant. Because we live in a universe where there is an *endless supply of energy*, which is the building block from which all things originate, there is enough—and there will always be enough—for every one of us to thrive. Creative energy is unlimited and continuously regenerated into the physical world. It is everywhere—an infinite sea of plenty. In other words, there is no limit to the amount of love, vitality, joy, or material abundance that we can create, enjoy, and experience. Why? Because at our core, we are all created from potential energy, of which there is a limitless supply, and this unlimited potentiality is available to each one of us in every moment. In his classic *The Abundance Book*, John Randolph Price writes:

> Since the beginning of the civilized world, enlightened ones have taught that prosperity is part of the natural process of life, and that lavish abundance is the unquestionable nature of each individual... The secret is to be aware of this unfailing principle, to understand that lack is simply the outpicturing of false beliefs, and to know that as you make the correction in consciousness, you will become a channel for the activity of ever-expanding influence in your life.[2]

There is simply no shortage of anything in the universe and more than enough for everyone to have our needs met and our desires fulfilled. So what's different about a woman who embodies the Law of Sufficiency and Abundance and one who still operates from lack? Let's look at a couple of real-life examples.

The professional woman who sees herself and her life as lacking complains that she can never meet any "good" men because she spends all her time traveling. The abundant woman, fueled by a similar desire to find her soul mate, finds traveling for business fun and exciting because

---

[2] John Randolph Price, *The Abundance Book* (Carlsbad, CA: Hay House, 2005), ix.

spending time in airplanes and airports is a great opportunity to meet fabulous, enterprising, available men.

The woman viewing her earning capacity from a lack perspective laments that even today women make an average of eighty cents to every man's dollar. The abundant woman doesn't concern herself with how much money others make; she focuses her attention toward enriching her creative capacity, which will probably earn her a raise.

The woman living in insufficiency and lack struggles to juggle her life's commitments and always feels as though she doesn't have enough time or energy to get it all done. She thinks of all the things she *has* to do and feels burdened. "I have to run to the bank and deposit checks. I have to pick up the kids from school. I have to go to work. I have to clean the house." The woman grounded in abundance thinks of all the things she *gets* to do and feels grateful. "I have all these checks that I get to deposit. I have beautiful, healthy children that I get to pick up from school. I have a job that supports me financially. I have a home that I get to care for." She takes stock of her full and active life and feels blessed. She is truly a nourished person, so she can express herself as a mother, a lover, a career woman, and a friend—she is energized, rather than overwhelmed, by these interactions. Life for her is full yet exciting and fulfilling.

The woman who views herself as lacking will inevitably (whether she speaks it out loud or not) assess a situation from the standpoint of *"What's in it for me?"* Because she is so uncertain of her own worthiness and skeptical of her ability to generate the affluence she requires, she is incapable of thinking beyond the scope of her immediate needs and whether or not they will be met. Unfortunately, this mindset imprisons her in less-than-satisfactory life experiences. She's simply too concerned with what she can take from any encounter to consider what she may be in a position to give. Her deepest contributions remain ungiven and she remains unfulfilled.

On the other hand, the woman who knows that she is an intricate part of an abundant universe approaches opportunities, both personal and professional, from the standpoint of *"How can I serve?"* Acutely aware of all her unique talents as well as all her blessings, giving is an act that comes completely natural to her. In this sense, she is a natural leader because she can consider the needs of others in addition to her own. Because she is capable of big-picture thinking and is not enslaved by an "all about me" mentality, opportunities are made available to her that never even register on the radar of the woman who is focused solely on self-preservation. Perhaps it is an answer to a question she's been pondering that falls right into her lap, a friend calls out of the blue telling her about a fantastic caterer just when she was planning a big party, or she sits next to a businesswoman at lunch who connects her with the perfect person to coordinate an upcoming event.

The Femininely Empowered Woman embodies abundance. She knows that the creative force is always available, flowing to and radiating through her and appearing as all forms of prosperity. She understands that the wellspring of abundance resides within her; it is not a place she arrives at by shoving others out of her way or through aggressive tactics. She's not trying to make things happen. She simply aligns herself with the abundance that is within her and attracts people and circumstances that appear at exactly the right time with the perfect solution to what she needs.

This woman knows that as a creative being, she is *always* creating or attracting to herself. This is an abundant universe and it will always give her, in great quantity, what she is sending out through her vibrations. It will either give her an abundance of *success*, if that is where her energy is attuned, or it will give her an abundance of *misfortunes*! She knows beyond a shadow of a doubt that she is dictating what she receives in life through her core beliefs.

> *This woman knows that as a creative being, she is* always *creating or attracting to herself. This is an abundant universe and it will always give her, in great quantity, what she is sending out through her vibrations.*

When we have an abundant mentality, we know *that there will always be enough and that the universe is benevolent.* We feel excited, certain that our needs will always be met at the perfect time. Even if what we expect doesn't come through, we know that the timing just wasn't right and something better is on its way.

An abundant mentality allows us to see the people in our lives as friendly and supportive team members and partners. We know that our family and friends have our backs and our best interests at heart. We don't get mired in jealousy toward others because we know that their attainments open the doors of possibility for all to attain. In fact, anything we can possibly dream for ourselves is ours to claim in the boundless universe in which we live.

Most importantly, when we shift into sufficiency and abundance, we perceive *ourselves* as whole and complete. We know at our core that who we are and what we have is enough. We feel enthused about the possibilities that await us in our future and expect all good things to come to us. We feel excited, expansive, and empowered.

The chart that follows summarizes what we attract, create, and experience when we operate in lack and limitation, and what is possible for us when we make the shift in consciousness to sufficiency and abundance.

	When Operating from Lack and Limitation	When Embracing Sufficiency and Abundance
How We Perceive Life	• Hostile • Limited resources • Filled with struggle and obstacles • Bleak future • Unfair • Financially challenging	• Overflowing with opportunities and resources • Friendly • Pleasant and surprising • Financially stable • Exciting • Endless possibilities
How We Perceive Others	• Withholding • Hurtful • Mean-spirited • Antagonistic	• Generous • Supportive • Helpful
	continued on next page ...	

	When Operating from Lack and Limitation	When Embracing Sufficiency and Abundance
		continued . . .
How Others Perceive Us	• Fear-based • Rigid • Insecure • Desperate • Ineffective	• Open • Secure • Confident • Resourceful • Carefree
How We Feel	• Powerless • Alone • Afraid • Insecure • Angry	• Fulfilled • Grateful and appreciative • Joyful • Empowered • Free

When you really grasp the advantages of operating from a state of abundance—not just as an intellectual concept but as something you embody—you'll no longer be tempted to use your energy forcing, coercing, demanding, or competing with anyone else in order to claim your share of the things you desire. You'll trust that if a desire exists in your heart, the potential for its fulfillment also exists and is part of your birthright. Changing your thoughts and beliefs may seem daunting, if not impossible, but consider this: it takes more energy to uphold limiting beliefs than it does to shift them.

When you can love who you are in this moment and appreciate all that you have, while at the same time feel excited for the things you will experience in the future, you are in perfect alignment with the Law of Sufficiency and Abundance.

Changing your thoughts and beliefs may seem daunting, if not impossible, but consider this: it takes more energy to uphold limiting beliefs than it does to shift them.

Fulfillment: The Key to Activating the Law of Sufficiency and Abundance

The secret to activating the Law of Sufficiency and Abundance is to become skilled at imagining and feeling as if what you desire is already yours. In other words, the longing is already fulfilled. The act of *wanting* something—whether a job with great benefits, a home that is impeccably organized, or a husband who is both passionate and faithful—ensures that the outcome you desire remains always "out there" in the future. Why? Because wanting indicates that you don't currently possess what you desire—it is something that you hope to get. So we tell the universe through thought and vibration that we lack what we desire. By now we know that the universe responds to our every thought, mirroring the beliefs we send out. For instance, if we want a new job and we remain in the vibration of longing, that is precisely what gets communicated to the universe. "Got it," the universe says. "You lack a new job. Your wish is my command. I grant you the lack of a new job (exactly as you expressed) and will continue to give you the lack of a new job for as long as you keep telling me that you lack a new job."

But if instead you cultivate the feeling that your desire has already been fulfilled, you magnetize that outcome to yourself far more powerfully than you ever could by wishing and longing for it. Your communication to the universe through the vibration of fulfillment goes something like this: "I am thrilled that my new job is on its way!" The universe mirrors back the vibration you are emitting and offers "like" energies in the form of your life experience—a new and rewarding job. See the subtle but profound distinction?

So how can you use this key to shift from a mindset of lack to one of abundance? First, you identify what you desire. Then you ask yourself, "How will I *feel* once this desire is fulfilled?" So if, for example, you're longing to meet your soul mate, imagine you are resting in his arms right now. How do you feel? Loved? Appreciated? Seen? Beautiful? Whatever the feeling is, feel it now, fully.

The trick is to live and breathe the outcome you desire *as if it's already here*. The more you do this, the easier it will be and the more real it will feel. This isn't about simply visualizing what you want. It's choosing to really *feel* your desire as already attained and to then sit back and allow the universe to do the heavy lifting by orchestrating the details for you. As bestselling author Marianne Williamson wrote in her book *A Return to Love: Reflections on the Principles of a Course in Miracles*, "Living out of our vision is more powerful than living out of our circumstance. Holding on to a vision invokes the circumstances by which the vision is achieved. Vision is content; material circumstances mere form."[3]

If you would love to live in financial affluence, take the time to imagine in 3D Technicolor what it would feel like to have more money than you could possibly spend. Would you feel excited? Vindicated? Relieved? Feel that now. Feel it with focus and passion and it will breathe life into your desire. Feel it as if you already have it, and it will be magnetized to you.

The outer world of circumstances and experiences is a reflection of your inner world of thoughts and feelings. Remember the equation from earlier? The more satisfied and appreciative you are of the life that you have, the more those satisfying and fulfilling experiences will be magnetized to you. This simple shift will radically alter your point of attraction: where you were once driven by anxiety, you are now fueled by excitement. Instead of obsessing over what you want (which leaves you in a perpetual state of *wanting*), you focus on and appreciate what you already have. You begin to trust that you have everything you need within you—right now—to build a fortune and reach your goals. You have all you need inside of you to create your ideal career. You have everything you need to attract the love of your life. From the knowledge that you already *are* enough, you call forth the experience of *having* enough.

Remember that abundance is an unending stream of well-being that is always available to you. This shift in consciousness will not only deliver you an immediate feeling

---

[3] Marianne Williamson, *A Return to Love: Reflections on the Principles of A Course in Miracles* (New York: Harper Collins, 1992), 186.

From the knowledge that you already are enough, you call forth the experience of having enough.

of relief but will also place you in the best possible position to magnetize all that you desire. The following journal exercise will support you in making this shift from insufficiency to abundance.

EXERCISE

Transforming Lack and Limitations into Sufficiency and Abundance

Set aside twenty to thirty minutes of uninterrupted time to complete this exercise. Make sure that you have a journal or a piece of paper and pen nearby to record any insights or actions that may arise.

To begin, allow yourself to recall a recent experience that triggered feelings of scarcity. Maybe you perceived yourself as lacking the talent or charisma to succeed in a project at work, or felt unsure that you would earn enough money to pay your bills. Allow the situation to arise in your mind, and see if you can replay it as if it were happening in this moment. As vividly as you can, picture the people involved in the situation and the circumstances that led up to it. Where were you? What were you doing? Be as honest as you can with yourself and write down whatever details you can recall.

See if you can recall what you were feeling in that moment. Give yourself permission to be vulnerable and to feel the underlying fears, doubts, uncertainties, and insecurities that triggered this experience. Ask yourself, "What was I afraid of?" and allow yourself to hear whatever answer arises. Perhaps you were feeling that opportunities were limited; that love or friendship was in short supply; or that you lacked the education, training, or experience to advance in your career.

Now give yourself permission to go a little deeper and identify the thoughts that triggered your emotions of insufficiency and inadequacy. Take your time and write down as many thoughts as you can recall.

See if you can follow these thoughts back to the core belief that ignited this thinking of lack and limitation. Be patient, simply allowing the belief to reveal itself in perfect time. How do you feel when you hold this belief in your awareness? Does it make you feel anxious, angry, contracted, or scared? Describe what you experience when you affirm this limiting belief and write it in your journal.

As you consider this underlying belief, ask yourself what new belief you could hold that would make you feel safe and secure. To feel worthy or valuable, prosperous or successful. What statements could you affirm that would lead to more empowering behaviors? Try these out and see how they feel:

* *All of my needs are met with ease at the perfect time.*

* *The universe is a rich and abundant place.*
* *Abundance flows to me continuously from many unexpected sources.*

Write down your new belief in your journal and allow it to become deeply anchored in your consciousness by saying it a few times out loud. Allow yourself to fully embody the meaning of this statement.

Ask yourself what actions you could take—right now or in the future—to align your behaviors with this new belief statement. Write down whatever ideas come to you. Allow yourself to feel the way you would feel if you actually took those actions. Would you feel excited? Alive? Proud? Relieved? Savor this feeling and allow it to wash over you, knowing that the more deeply you integrate it into your mind and heart, the more magnetic it will become.

And with your next breath, consciously and deliberately release any thoughts or feelings of lack and limitation, and allow yourself to feel completely free and invigorated as you feel the fulfillment of your desire having already appeared.

• • • • • • • • • • • • • •

Go to www.alphabitchbook.com to download an additional meditation on abundance, and use the authorization code TYABFREE.

Bitch Tip

If you are spiraling into lack, or feeling envious of what others have, ask yourself, "What are five things I can appreciate about myself and my life as they exist *right now*?"

From Alpha Bitch to Femininely Empowered Woman

As women, we find ourselves once again at the dawn of a revolution. This one has nothing to do with asserting our autonomy or embracing our sexuality…we're already well established in these areas. Unlike prior awakenings that altered how others perceived us as women, this one is happening deep within each of us. As we learn to accomplish our goals—not by wielding aggressive masculine energy but by drawing upon our authentic feminine power—our experience of life changes radically. We are every bit as focused, determined, and successful as our Alpha counterparts, but we're also more relaxed and at ease. Instead of exhausting ourselves and others by feverishly trying to *make* things happen, we become skilled in the art of attuning our thoughts and emotions with the universal laws that govern manifestation.

By embracing *the Law of Pure Potentiality*, we realize that we don't have to use force to be effective. Instead, we can tap into Source energy—which created us and everything in the universe—and allow it to direct the fulfillment of our intentions.

To activate *the Law of Allowing*, we need only surrender our addiction to control. As we become softer and more yielding, we invite abundance, love, and unforeseen opportunities to flow freely in and out of our lives.

The Law of Oneness reminds us that we are far more powerful when our energies are aligned in collaboration than when they are opposed in competition. Viewing others not as threats but as sources of inspiration builds a sense of community between us that fosters support and mutual prosperity.

The Law of Balance and Harmony guides us to search for inner peace and tranquility, rather than giving in to discord and opposition. By letting go of drama, our creative energies become more focused and our results are amplified.

And finally, by embracing *the Law of Sufficiency and Abundance*, we see solutions where we once saw only problems, and opportunities where none seemed to exist before. Because we are focused on what we can give, rather than on what we can take, we become conduits of what is truly an endless supply of resources.

By making the choice to abandon the fruitless quest for dominance and superiority, you gain the power to tune out the comparing, competing, fear-based mental chatter that keeps you from enjoying your life experiences as they unfold. And because you no longer squander your energy trying to exert influence over other people, you are more mentally focused and physically vibrant, and have an ample

supply of energy available to
fund your own creations.

As a woman who has
learned to access the feminine power within you, you
have the tools to sustain
yourself from within. Your
well of confidence runs deep
because it's based upon your

*You are the woman with the
"It" factor—that certain
magical something that is
hard to define yet impossible
to ignore.*

innate value and not on accomplishments or positions that
are fleeting at best. You're no longer tempted to go out dig-
ging for "bones," whether in the form of validation, adora-
tion, or monetary rewards because you understand that the
real source of all that you crave is within you.

By nurturing your feminine side and giving it permission
to come forth, you radiate a calm, commanding presence that
draws others in.

You are the woman with the "It" factor—that certain
magical something that is hard to define yet impossible to
ignore. Life becomes seamless and flowing. The quality of
the people you attract increases, as does the quality of the
interactions, projects, and experiences that you enjoy with
those people.

Perhaps the most immediate reward of replacing primitive Alpha Bitch behaviors with a Femininely Empowered
Woman approach is that it affords you greater control over
your thoughts and emotions. Desperation, worry, urgency,
and bossiness no longer find a home within your energetic
field as you become more adept in maintaining a vibration
that is high and clear. With practice, you develop the ability

to maintain your composure and stay grounded in your center—even when other Alpha females are busy creating chaos or trying to enroll you in their dramas.

"Beware of Dog"

Most of the complaints we hear from women who operate in Alpha mode are centered on their encounters with other Alpha females. One of the most encouraging signs that you are evolving beyond this mindset and into a more balanced and empowered consciousness is when you begin to develop the ability to sidestep these potential altercations. So what will you do the next time you encounter an Alpha she-wolf—whether at work or in your own family—who has teeth bared and is ready for battle?

The first step is to recognize the futility of going up against her, resisting her, competing with her, or engaging in her drama by remembering that fear, jealousy, and competition only constrict the amount of love and abundance that you're capable of receiving. With a few deep breaths, remind yourself that kindness is infinitely more effective than cruelty and affirm that your calm demeanor is a reflection of your deliberate and powerful choosing, not a sign of weakness or apathy. When you feel your mood beginning to degenerate from faith to fear or from composure to competitiveness, perform one of the exercises presented throughout this book or log on to our website, www.tamingyouralphabitch.com, for an instant energy upgrade.

Rather than lashing out at the person or situation that triggered the feelings within you, do your best to trace them back to the thoughts and beliefs that ignited them from within. By following the manifestation formula back to its source, you can disarm the "bomb" before it detonates.

Sometimes our Alpha behavior seems to erupt out of nowhere in response to a particular person or situation, while at other times it arises out of a chronic mindset. But regardless of how it shows up or how long it has been operating, if you're willing to follow the example we're showing you here, you can regroup, realign your energies, and chart a new course for yourself. Our client Moira was generous enough to give us permission to share her experience.

Moira is a top executive at a successful corporation who enjoys power, prestige, and the sizeable paychecks that come along with the title. Although she could be abrupt at times, she was known for producing results and was looked upon by senior partners as the "right man for the job." By all outer appearances, Moira had it all: a lucrative career, a handsome husband, and a beautiful little boy. But for all that she had achieved, inside she felt like she was falling apart. When she was at work, she felt anxious; when she came home, she felt on edge and angry.

Like so many of us, Moira had adopted an Alpha Bitch persona that enabled her to keep pace in a male-dominated profession and manage the logistics of juggling a career while running a household and raising a young child. Every morning, she suited up in her Alpha Bitch combat gear, her inner warrior poised with sword drawn and ready for battle. Unfortunately, this posture became her habitual way of relating, and not just when she was at work; it also followed her home to her husband and son, with whom she was becoming increasingly demanding and short-tempered. By the time she gave herself the gift of a much-needed Goddess Retreat, she was showing serious signs of battle fatigue.

During her weekend away, without the thick armor that kept people at a distance, Moira's entire presence began to change. She looked softer and she smiled more. Without the weight of the world on her shoulders, we all got a chance to appreciate her thoughtful insights and her fabulous sense of humor. After the retreat ended, she devoted herself to making the transformation from Alpha Bitch to Femininely Empowered Woman.

When she returned home, her first task was to simply catch herself whenever she started slipping into a "dog-eat-dog" stance; since presenting herself as tough and capable had been Moira's mission in life, this was relatively easy. Next, she was to connect with the emotions that were present whenever she acted out in aggressive, controlling, or untrusting ways. As you might guess, fear and inadequacy were identified as the primary sources. She feared that she wouldn't be appreciated unless she fought hard to keep winning titles. She feared that she would be hurt if she didn't keep her guard up at all times, and that she would never amount to anything if she didn't push herself to her limits in order to achieve. Most of all, she feared that she wouldn't be loved unless she proved that she was the best at everything. No wonder she had been feeling so emotionally depleted and defeated!

Having identified the feelings that sent her spinning into Alpha mode, Moira then tuned into the habitual thoughts that went hand in hand with these fears and uncovered a deluge: *So much is expected of me, how will I pull it off?... I don't have enough time to get everything done... What did I forget to do today?* A theme quickly emerged, one that is common to nearly every Alpha female: underneath all her ambition and hyper-rigid scheduling, Moira felt that she was inadequate to meet the expectations of those around her. As she admitted how many times each day thoughts like these were being broadcast through her mind, her shoulders slumped under the weight of the realization.

Moira began to recall the messages she had received from parents, teachers, former bosses, and even friends: *You're only as good as your grades. People won't respect you if you don't achieve. There is no room for second best. You can rest when you're dead.* To help her appreciate how counterproductive these beliefs actually were to her happiness and well-being, we asked Moira to speculate how effective one of her employees would be if they had to function in the midst of this kind of negativity. Of course, when she imagined someone other than herself trying to cope in the presence of such limiting beliefs, she instantly saw how destructive it would be.

Next came the task of replacing those disparaging, outdated beliefs with healthier and more productive ones—new belief statements that were self-loving and accepting. As time went by, the more naturally these new beliefs reverberated through her mind and heart and rolled off her tongue, the better she felt and the lighter she became. The stern, hard edge that had concealed her true self began to soften, and a kinder, more loving person emerged. As she made it a priority to reconnect with the sensitive and caring side of her, she realized how much she longed for more intimacy with others and for more tranquility within herself. Fulfilling this desire became her new goal.

Of course, dropping her tough-girl facade doesn't always come easy for Moira. At times it feels extremely scary and she feels vulnerable. But luckily, we Alphas are not lacking in determination or courage, and neither is Moira! She was committed to being softer, quieter, and more centered within herself, and it wasn't long before she noticed some pretty remarkable results.

One day a male coworker she didn't get along with paused to open the door for her. Feeling genuinely moved by this simple act, she took a moment to engage her younger colleague in a conversation, and created a rapport that translated into a more harmonious working relationship between the two. Her son, who used to avoid her whenever she walked into the house, now calls her during the day just to say "hi" and comes out of his room to hug her when she comes home from work. Her husband smiles at her more and goes out of his way to do special things for her. She blushed when she told us that allowing herself to feel feminine seems to be bringing out the man in him.

Encouraged by how differently people are responding to her—and by how much better she feels inside her own skin—Moira remains committed to chipping away at the guard that took her years to construct. When anxiety or irritation surface now, which they do from time to time, she takes this as a little nudge that reminds her to let go, trust, and reconnect with her femininity. Moira considers herself a "work in progress," but every day that she chooses to bring alanced, and theout.

* * *

Like Moira, we are all a work in progress. The forceful
Miranda Priestlys, the controlling Miranda Hobbeses, the
competitive Monica Gellers, the disruptive Scarlett O'Haras,
and, of course, the reality-show divas that we see every day
on television and in movies continuously tell our inner Alpha that she is on the right track to world domination. It's
hard to step away from center stage long enough to ask ourselves, "At what cost am I getting what I want?" Sure, Miranda Priestly had a great career, but all of her employees hated
her. Yes, the "Housewives" have hit television shows and
fifteen minutes of fame, but at what cost to their dignity?
When Alpha Bitch mode takes over, as we've demonstrated
throughout this book, you can get pretty far—far away from
your true feminine authenticity, that is.

Hopefully you can now recognize that the Alpha Bitch
is a dying female breed; her aggression takes more energy to
generate than is possible to keep going, and she is outlived
(physically and emotionally) by her wiser Femininely Empowered Woman counterpart. It is time that we start looking
to the women who are leaders in the revolution of feminine
power—women who command respect because of who they
are, not because of the aggressive, controlling, or competitive
ways in which they attained their accomplishments.

Most importantly, it's time to start looking at ourselves
as examples of strong, graceful, empowered women. By us-

ing the tools provided here, you can awaken the Feminine Power within you and start to evolve your life into something you *create*, and do it exactly the way you were intended: with ease, fluidity, and grace.

acknowledgments

We are so grateful to the invaluable contributions of our family, friends, and colleagues. Your support and guidance have made this journey possible.

To Danielle Dorman: we are ever grateful (and constantly amazed) at your editorial genius. Where would we be without you? It's a question we often ask ourselves—and one we hope never to put to the test. Thank you for your extraordinary dedication.

To Glenn Yeffeth and the team at BenBella Books: you embody the true meaning of collaboration. We can't thank you enough for working *with* us every step of the way.

To Celeste Fine and Folio Literary Management: thank you for never giving up on the vision.

To Jacquie Jordan and the group at TVGuestperts: thank you for your encouragement, guidance, and sass!

To the amazing goddesses who have shared their lives and light with us: we are so grateful to you.

To our "goddess team" who helps us in countless ways at the retreats: we love you and thank you. Especially Evelyn Apostolou, you are a true manifestation of the goddess and are our "blessing."

To all the authors who offered their kind words to this project: we are so grateful.

From Rebecca

To Mom, Dad, Irene, and Gil: thank you for showing me what love, loyalty, and unwavering devotion look like. I am so blessed to be part of our family.

To Charlie, Alex, and Brianna: thank you for standing *by* me and *with* me, no matter what! We definitely put the "fun" in dysfunctional, and I wouldn't have it any other way.

To Alex: thank you for "choosing me"! You fill my life with incomparable joy and lightness. I am always delighted to be in your presence and feel so blessed to share this life with you.

And to Brianna: from the moment you were born I have been captivated by your extraordinary beauty and grace. Every day you teach me what it means to be a true goddess—powerful and poised, fierce and feminine. I stand in awe of you.

To my soul sisters Jill Lebeau and Mary Mohs: your ever-present love and support throughout our many years together have been deeply nourishing. I am so blessed to call you my friends.

To Christy: you are such an amazing teacher of abundance, and I am so grateful to you for encouraging me to "up my game"! I appreciate all that you've brought into my life!

From Christy

To the amazing men in my life: Frederic, Alexander, and Maxim—I love you so much.

To the most amazing coauthor, partner, and friend: Rebecca Grado, you are my *soul sister*. There are not enough words to express my gratitude for you.

To Jonathan Hunsaker, aka "Big Daddy": without you, my dreams would not be a reality. You are the wind beneath my wings—and the only person who can stand my singing voice. Thank you does not say enough.

To Sharon DiStaulo: the best assistant ever!

To the One Net Marketing team, especially Terri Romine: you are the nuts and bolts of my business. Without you and your amazing team at One Net Marketing, I couldn't do what I do.

To Brendon Burchard: you are a true mentor and coach. Your guidance and support are so appreciated.

A big thank-you to all the QSCA coaches whom I consider family!

about the authors

REBECCA GRADO, MFT, is a licensed psychotherapist and author. She holds a master's degree in counseling and a bachelor's degree in clinical psychology. For the past twenty-five years, she has maintained a thriving private practice where she has helped thousands of individuals transcend limitations, discover their innate power and joy, and awaken their greatest potential. She has been studying metaphysics since 1985 and is a visionary in her approach to energy work and healing. Rebecca is also the cofounder of the Goddess Retreat. She inspires women every day to create their greatest success with ease and grace. As a gifted writer, Rebecca's work has been featured with bestselling authors Dr. Wayne Dyer and Anthony Robbins. She resides in the San Francisco Bay Area with her son, Alex, and daughter, Brianna.

CHRISTY WHITMAN is an in-demand life coach, transformational leader, CEO and founder of the Quantum Success Coaching Academy. She helps thousands of women and men around the world achieve their goals through her empowerment seminars, speeches, coaching sessions, and products. Christy's life-changing message reaches more than 81,000 people a month, and she has been quoted in *Seventeen*, *Woman's World*, *Woman's Day*, *Teen Vogue*, *The Star-Ledger*, and *The Knot Magazine*. As a certified Law of Attraction coach, her work has been promoted by and featured with bestselling authors like Marianne Williamson, Dr. Wayne Dyer, and Marci Shimoff. She lives in Montreal with her husband, Frederic, and their two boys, Alexander and Maxim.